"Kelly Minter writes with a maturity beyond her years. This book was a pleasure to read because of her keen insight, raw honesty, rich use of colorful imagery, and clever turns of phrase. *Water into Wine* is two books in one—and both are good. It's the story of a young artist's journey to and through the music industry of Nashville; it's also the story of a soul's pilgrimage to the heart of God. Jesus's first miracle is cleverly unpacked as an excellent metaphor for spiritual transformation—Kelly's and ours."

—GARY W. MOON, professor of counseling and
spirituality at the Psychological Studies Institute
and author of *Falling for God*

"Kelly Minter is a refreshing new voice for those of us who want to honor God but must also laugh at our humanity. With humor and kindness, *Water into Wine* invites every last drop of your heart to be given to the One who loves perfectly. I am, to use Kelly's words, *filled to the brim* for having read this lovely work."

—JAN MEYERS, author of *Listening to Love*

"This book is a beautiful reminder that sweet fruit grows in the rich soil of humility and obedience."

—LISA HARPER, Bible teacher and author
of *Every Woman's Hope*

"In *Water into Wine,* Kelly Minter embodies her fresh and sometimes astonishing insights in the relatable stuff of everyday life, making her both an excellent teacher and a welcome companion on the Way."

—CAROLYN ARENDS, recording artist and author

WATER *into* WINE

*Hope for the Miraculous
in the Struggle of the Mundane*

KELLY MINTER

WATERBROOK
PRESS

WATER INTO WINE
PUBLISHED BY WATERBROOK PRESS
2375 Telstar Drive, Suite 160
Colorado Springs, CO 80920
A division of Random House, Inc.

ISBN 1-57856-797-1

Library of Congress Cataloging-in-Publication Data
Minter, Kelly.
  Water into wine : hope for the miraculous in the struggle of the mundane / Kelly Minter.
     p. cm.
  ISBN 1-57856-797-1
  1. Turning water into wine at the wedding at Cana (Miracle)—Meditations. 2. Christian life—Meditations. I. Title.
BT367 .M37M55 2004
232.9'55—dc22   2004002067

Printed in the United States of America
2004—First Edition

10 9 8 7 6 5 4 3 2 1

*To Mom and Dad—for being living examples
of the water-into-wine transformation*

CONTENTS

ACKNOWLEDGMENTS

I am desperately grateful for the blessing of the following relationships, knowing that because of you, I am as rich as I could ever be…

To Don Pape, publisher at WaterBrook Press—Your belief in me, and in this book, is something that I simply cannot put words to. Thank you for giving me my first shot at "author," for being a fantastic publisher, and especially for being a friend.

To Elisa Fryling Stanford, for your steadfast oversight and persistence in seeing this book to its end.

To my editor, Traci Mullins of Eclipse Editorial Services—If ever there was a case for providential meetings, we are it! Thanks for preserving my voice, stretching my craft, and somehow making it all look like a book. (And to Trixie, for being a new friend.)

To my manager, Pamela Muse, for several years of hard work and belief—it's a blessing to journey with you.

To Dennis Disney, Ryan Howard, and the Howards, for giving me my second shot at "recording artist."

To KC and Cyndi for your relentless prayers.

To Al Andrews of Porter's Call for being a timely compass.

Tonia—Thanks for being along for the process and for providing me with friendship and thus a wealth of content for books to come.

April—Your friendship and lightness are gifts I would never want to live without.

To Margaret, for a friendship that influences and shapes my thoughts and writings—Don't go anywhere.

Kim and Jim Thomas of The Village Chapel—I am home.

To my amazing grandparents, Charles and Mary Minter and David and Elizabeth Cowen, for life and love itself.

Most of all, to my parents, Mike and Kay, and to my sisters and brother, Megan, Katie, and David—Without you, this book would never be.

FOREWORD

There is a continual coming of age in matters of faith for each of us. It is a painful process that requires nothing less than everything. It is not for the weak or the faint at heart. It is not for the follower.

This coming of age, when embraced, is a beautiful journey that takes years to begin and, I suspect, an entire lifetime to complete. But its evidences are undeniable when they are played out in people. Among the most noticeable are humility and trust: the ability to remain weak and the will to remain strong despite weakness.

So seemingly incongruous, these two traits. Humility: the posture of a seeker, a student—someone who does not need to know everything to feel whole, but rather, who finds wholeness in the pursuit of knowledge. Trust: belief beyond the visible and the clearly determined. Both are necessary for a successful discipleship journey.

These pages hold the evidences of a spiritual coming of age, a glimpse of one section on the long road toward Christ-like character. They contain the treasures of a beautiful and fierce struggle, a journey marked by humility and trust, a journey well taken.

It is a journey that most of us shy away from. It is so much easier to glean what someone else has discovered than to take that reckless journey alone. So very easy, and safe, because if what we are told to do turns out to be bad information, well, it could never be *our fault*—after all, we were *only doing what we were told*.

But I suspect true discipleship requires much more than reliving someone else's experience. It requires our presence, our full participation. It requires listening intently through one's own questions and inequities. It requires careful following, with raw, barefooted steps, and patient waiting in the midst of the riddles. There can be no judgment, no premature relief. I am sure that it is infinitely more difficult to be a disciple than a follower.

In these pages you will find a disciple, someone who is moving and breathing according to a careful pursuance of her God and his unique will for her. In Kelly's story you will find a beautiful grid, a template for your own journey. The markers will differ I am sure, but the end result—to become more like Christ, to accept his individual will for your life, to live with a curious mystery, a divine riddle at times—will be synonymous.

Water into Wine is a metaphor for the discipleship journey. It is a long process filled with bittersweet change. It takes a lot to pour out the water of your experience before God and expect him to lead you to the finer beauty of it, and even more, to allow the fermentation of your experience to transform into the precious wine of his presence.

But it is precisely that process that deposits us at the most irresistible truth of the cross—the unfathomable love that it took to endure it. That love, given to us by Christ, is the kind of love that cares enough to patiently grow each of us into completion, despite our kicking and groaning, despite our blindness and failings.

I am certain that as you journey through this book, you will feel Christ bend low to his creation and whisper, *"Won't you come journey with me? I have so many things to tell you."*

And I am even more certain that you will be empowered by the telling.

—MARGARET BECKER, songwriter and recording artist

On the third day a wedding took place at Cana in Galilee. Jesus' mother was there, and Jesus and his disciples had also been invited to the wedding. When the wine was gone, Jesus' mother said to him, "They have no more wine."

"Dear woman, why do you involve me?" Jesus replied, "My time has not yet come."

His mother said to the servants, "Do whatever he tells you."

Nearby stood six stone water jars, the kind used by the Jews for ceremonial washing, each holding from twenty to thirty gallons.

Jesus said to the servants, "Fill the jars with water"; so they filled them to the brim.

Then he told them, "Now draw some out and take it to the master of the banquet."

They did so, and the master of the banquet tasted the water that had been turned into wine. He did not realize where it had come from, though the servants who had drawn the water knew. Then he called the bridegroom aside and said, "Everyone brings out the choice wine first and then the cheaper wine after the guests have had too much to drink; but you have saved the best till now."

This, the first of his miraculous signs, Jesus performed at Cana in Galilee. He thus revealed his glory, and his disciples put their faith in him.

—JOHN 2:1–12

INTRODUCTION

YOU ARE INVITED...

Weddings. I remember tagging along to them with my parents when I was a kid. At the time they felt a lot more like cumbersome activities weighing down my weekends than sacred celebrations. The couples who planned early morning ceremonies never seemed to factor in my Saturday morning cartoon schedule. And those who were slated to tie the knot in the afternoon never took into account my weekly kickball games at the end of the cul-de-sac.

Of course, it was only the actual ceremony that I really dreaded; the reception was a different story. I got good at knowing that the latter was where a seemingly endless supply of snacks and desserts made its appearance. It was also where I became free to run around, commiserating with my other unfortunate friends who had found themselves in the same weekend boat.

Fortunately, I grew out of this nonappreciative stage around the same time that cartoons began to lose their appeal and kickball was replaced with high-school jerseys. Romance, simultaneously, became a budding interest of mine, and something about honoring two people's love for each other at an extravagant party seemed more and more captivating. I even began to enjoy dressing up for such occasions, seriously regarding my role as a witness to the union of close friends. Eventually I was surprised by the fact that the ceremonies had topped the receptions in my mental tiers of importance.

Despite this evolution in my thinking, there is one ceremony I would have skipped altogether if only I could have experienced its surrounding subplots. To catch a glimpse of Jesus, his glory as well as his humanity. To bear the stone jars that housed miracles. To watch Mary gracefully mingle influence with submission. To brush shoulders with humble servants who chose the lowly road but gained a sacred knowledge. And, of course, to sip wine that once was water…

Yes, I am speaking of the renowned wedding that took place at Cana in Galilee some two thousand years ago. Although I missed receiving an invitation by a mere score of centuries, I get the uncanny feeling that I was there. Perhaps it's because the scriptural account teems with characters who look strangely familiar. Characters who play you and me. And isn't it interesting that the whole motley crew takes the stage in the context of a celebration—and yet a dilemma; humble servants amidst honored guests; featuring the wine, but not apart from the water. This wedding presents us with a collision of paradoxes that make up what we know as "life."

An uphill road rarely paved with smooth surfaces; the journey is replete with steep angles and hairpin turns…but these ragged edges are the very elements God uses as refining agents in our lives. To ferment our faith, if you will. To aid us in becoming fine wine— wine that promises to get better with age. But only *if* we submit ourselves to the process. That's the fundamental premise. And I can't think of a better setting that relays this principle—at least insofar as it relates to my own spiritual quest—than the wedding where Jesus performed his first recorded miracle—turning water into wine.

The wedding is a centering location that reminds me that only God is capable of turning my earthy, ignoble offerings into something as divine as wine. It encourages me to take heart as I wade through the commonplace moments of life, knowing that the miraculous could be hiding beneath the mundane. It challenges me to obey and to serve (even though these words can make me squirm at times), recognizing the great rewards that come as a result. Mostly, Cana reminds me of the Jesus I serve—a merciful, all-powerful, water-into-wine-making Savior who is worth my all.

For precisely these reasons I invite you to drop in with me on a wedding that might be host to many of our own reflections. A wedding where we are free to impose on the characters, engage in their activities, and embrace some of their most defining moments. As we do this, however, I will give you fair warning that I am one for tangents and rabbit trails, so don't look for anything to be too linear. I'm also not very accomplished at making great sense of some of the loose ends that may be present, so I hope you're not too set on neatly wrapped packages; real life seems to be a bit messy anyhow. But no matter how far we travel off the beaten path, we will faithfully circle back to Cana for inspiration and perspective, but mostly for companionship.

Companionship, because it is here that we will find our own stories mirrored. It is here that we will catch glimpses of our own faces, questions, and puzzling riddles. Here we will rediscover the value of recognizing those things that transcend age and time, cultural and generational barriers. Things like the struggle of faith, the despair of disappointment, the agony that often accompanies obedience, the blessings of servanthood, the risks of trust, and the lure of the sparkling world. We will find comfort in the fact that today, more than two thousand years since this remarkable wedding, on a distant continent, in another era, and as members of a different race, we *still* find ourselves carrying water, encountering miracles, questioning Jesus, and finding him faithful in the end.

All this to say, you are cordially invited. To attend a wedding we missed the first time around, but one we'll soon discover we've danced at more times than we can imagine.

Come…be my guest.

I

TO THE BRIM

A dear friend of mine has a golden retriever named Max. I'm not all that keen on pets, but even I have to admit that he's just about the most likeable puppy you've ever seen. With a few energetic wags of his tail, he can feed any starving self-esteem that walks in the door. In Max's presence you can go from feeling friendless to mistaking yourself for a celebrity in a matter of wags.

If I can cite just one flaw with Max—and I'm really stretching here—it's that he doesn't play fair with the ball. Every time I branch out of my nonpet comfort zone and take him out for a game of fetch, I come back with the same warm slime coating my hands from having to reach into his mouth. I throw the ball, but when Max brings the ball back, he doesn't drop it. I resort to going in after it with my once germ-free fingers while he clenches it with his canine fangs. Hence, the problem: We're playing two different games! I see the ball, and it makes me want to play fetch; Max sees the ball, and it makes him want to play tug of war.

To date, Max and I haven't successfully resolved this issue. However, I recently witnessed a new friend visiting from New York make out in brilliant fashion when faced with my same predicament. When Max wouldn't release the ball, she started walking away and, with an impeccable New York accent, announced, "I yain't beggin'." Max immediately dropped the ball and got several more throws out of her.

I've tried to employ such techniques, and though I'm faring a bit better, I'm afraid my feigned "New Yawk" inflections aren't all that believable. Max still would rather play tug of war—and when it comes to my relationship with God, sometimes, so would I.

To say that I have had difficulty with surrender and obedience would be a profound understatement. To say that this struggle has sometimes left me feeling as if I might just fall over dead, or that every ounce of wind has been knocked out of me, comes a little bit closer. There's nothing easy about it, despite the "Trust and Obey" childlike melody, which could lead you to believe that it's a walk in the park. Because my own desires rarely point in the direction of surrender, I find myself pondering over and over again the obedience fork-in-the-road: *Do I go to the right—my way—or to the left—God's way?* Or, of course, I can always choose the ever-popular option of forging down the middle where there is no road, thinking that somehow this will satisfy both God and me. It's just that it never works out this way. I end up pleasing neither, and then realize that on top of everything else, I have missed out on the luxury of having a paved road under my feet. This is all part of the obedience dilemma; there is no middle road.

At Your Service

The word *servanthood* is right up there with *obedience* in my list of topics I surreptitiously avoid. I have regularly tensed up while listening to sermons or reading books regarding this subject, squirming in my chair, desperately hoping I wouldn't actually be "convicted" to *do* something.

My slight overreaction may stem from the fact that the idea of servanthood has been presented to me in dry and predictable fashions, over the course of my upbringing and travels, in the pews of more churches than I can count. Our contemporary Christian culture seems to have promoted the narrow definition of a servant as someone who faithfully teaches the first-grade Sunday-school class, cooks for the homeless once a month, volunteers for this or that, or assumes another's unwanted chores. Frankly, I have mostly felt burdened and depleted when trying to implement this brand of servanthood. In an attempt to remedy my guilty conscience, I have often latched onto some unappealing task—for which I have no gifting—and proceeded to hunker down under the burden of what I perceived to be the "servant" thing to do. This less-than-delightful process inevitably prompted silent groans of annoyance and resentment, as well as disappointment in myself for not being as wide-eyed and perky as all the other "servants" around me.

Over the past several years, I have been discovering a picture of servanthood that looks exceedingly different from what I once perceived. Turns out I've had it mostly wrong. Bottom line is that I had missed the very personal aspect of servanthood. I had fallen into the trap of serving a "system," not a person. But servanthood by its very nature requires that *someone* be served, which is why it is personal. Servanthood is about people, and ultimately about God, because God desperately loves people. We err when we make it about principles or ideals.

We see the Pharisees guilty of this at every turn in the Gospels: They were faithful to implement almost every form of service, yet Jesus made it clear that they were not serving him—and they certainly weren't serving people when they ruthlessly criticized him for healing the sick and helping the poor. The Pharisees were serving a religion, a belief system, a set of principles that gave them a false sense of righteousness. I have no idea how they kept it up, because, being guilty of similar things, I quickly burned out in my misguided attempts to serve at the altar of obligation rather than love. I am thrilled to be learning that servanthood is not supposed to work this way.

I was recently presented with further insight into this concept while sitting in church. My pastor, Jim, was teaching on another well-known story: Jesus's washing of the disciples' feet. Jim singled out a few verses that deeply challenged me.

Jesus knew that the Father had put all things under
his power, and that he had come from God and
was returning to God; so he got up from the meal,
took off his outer clothing, and wrapped a towel
around his waist. After that, he poured water into a
basin and began to wash his disciples' feet, drying
them with the towel that was wrapped around him.
(John 13:3-5)

Jim highlighted the important point that Jesus was confident
in his position. He knew that he had *everything;* he understood his
rightful place as one who had come from God and was going to
God. Therefore, he was free to lay aside his outer garments, serving his disciples in the humblest of ways.

Unlike Jesus, I am rarely confident of my position. I am afraid
of what I might lose if I serve, or if I prefer others above myself, or
if I allow someone to take a coveted place I would like for myself.
But on those occasions when I understand and fully believe that,
indeed, all is mine—all good gifts and Christ himself—I am free
to lay down my "garments," arise from the table at which I am
seated, and kneel down to wash the feet of my sisters and broth-
ers. I am free to serve, knowing that I will lose nothing of true
importance.

Usually, however, I find myself still clinging to too much. I
want a bit of notoriety. I don't mind serving, but I want to be noted
for it. I'm not great at operating in obscurity. If I'm going to take

the low place, I would at least like to be applauded for my humility (as much of an oxymoron as this is.)

As God continues to mend my negative feelings and misconceptions of what servanthood is really all about, I am finding that it's a lot less about doing and a lot more about being. It's not a list of things we sign up for; it's the spirit by which we live. It's a posture. Serving God or a person in the truest manner requires far more than volunteering for an event, penciling in our names for the church nursery shift, and driving carpools. It demands our hearts. It asks for everything we are. It is a great deal more costly than I ever imagined—and far more rewarding as well.

TUG OF WAR

T. S. Eliot said that most religious writing fails because the writers don't write about how they really feel; they write about how they *want* to feel. I will strive to offer you both. I will tell you in no uncertain terms how surrendering in the midst of my spiritual tugs of war has sometimes made me *feel,* but if you will indulge me further on this topic, I believe there are blessings to be discovered on the other end, blessings that reflect more of what I think we all *want*—the prospect of divine wine. In the pages that follow, I loosely refer to water and wine—*water* representing everything human and earthly; *wine* representing everything supernatural, righteous, miraculous, heavenly, God-breathed.

One of my last Max-like tug-of-war matches with God spanned

the course of several months, leaving me thoroughly worn out. I had taken the plunge and moved to Nashville, Tennessee, to continue pursuing my dream of being a recording artist and singer/songwriter. I had come to this town with eyes as wide as the ocean, dreams bigger than Dorothy's, and on a road I was certain was paved with yellow bricks. I was well aware that the competition was steep and the slots for rising stars were fewer than winning lottery tickets. But I also had a very deep desire to sing and to write and to have an impact; so no matter how daunting the challenges, I had to come.

In the summer of 1999, after many years of dreaming, I finally found myself coaxing my gun-metal-gray Jeep toward Nashville— I say "coaxing," because getting it here was a real feat. The thing could barely get in and out of my family's suburban Washington, D.C., neighborhood, much less into another state. But the Jeep was no less shaky than I, so we tried it together, my guitar and a few other possessions in tow. After driving a humid fourteen hours with no air conditioner and a burst water hose, I figured things had to be looking up when the highway began to straighten out in such a way that the trees on either side lined up like arrows pointing to what felt like the Promised Land. The curtain had been pulled back, and the Nashville skyline blazed with promise, as if cheering me toward home under the dark canopy of night. I had no reason to believe that things would not go exactly as I had planned.

I remember when my friend Nicole, who was working for my management company at the time, casually shared with me a disturbing possibility. In a short sentence she sent my set-in-stone plans spiraling like pieces of popcorn in a tornado. "Things might not end up looking the way you hope," she said matter-of-factly. This notion presented a significant problem for me because how I *hoped* things were going to look was nonnegotiable and didn't need any rearranging as far as I was concerned. I had the whole thing mapped out and though I had "surrendered" my plans to God, what I meant in my heart was that I would allow him to do what he needed to do as long as he worked within my general parameters.

Somehow this kind of surrender was not cutting it. I began to realize that I was clutching my career plans, counting them dearer than whatever God's plans might be for me. Commence the tug-of-war match! I couldn't bear the image of relinquishing my dreams to God. He had been asking for them all along, but the idea of unfolding my trembling fingers and allowing my own agenda to slip through the cracks felt like the death of me. My lack of trust in God had been exposed; I longed for wine, but I wanted to make it my own way.

RECKLESS OBEDIENCE

In stark contrast to my propensities to grasp things tightly, the servants at the wedding in Cana modeled an entirely different response that challenges everything I've believed about obedience. Their willingness to give Jesus all he asked for shines brightly against my reluctance to do the same, because when Jesus told the servants to fill the stone jars with water, Scripture tells us that they did so. As if this, in and of itself, isn't convicting enough, there is an additional detail that causes my insides to twist and turn in uneasy positions: Scripture goes on to say that they filled the jars "to the brim."

It's amazing how challenging three one-syllable words can be. These words speak volumes to me because I am one who would rather decide exactly how much obedience I would like to offer God, as opposed to the servants' no-holds-barred approach. As I have said, my own tendency would be to fill the jars halfway or, at best, just a few inches short of the lip, because with every inch that is left unfilled, I signify that which I consider still to be mine. Even if I am short only one drop, it's a drop difference between giving Him everything and nothing. And that chasm becomes no wider or slimmer, whether it's one drop or fifty. Which is why our agony tends to be so great when taking true steps of obedience.

I can only speculate as to whether the servants felt a similar agony, though I am persuaded that their obedience was much more difficult than what first meets the eye. The simple act of filling jars with water, alone, is not terribly impressive. But the fact that the wedding hosts had run out of wine, not water, puts a different spin on things. It gives added credence to the reckless obedience of the servants because it portrays their faithfulness to pour water when the crowd was looking for wine. Their response to Jesus's command seems ludicrous at best and tedious at worst.

In addition, I can't ignore the setting: a wedding celebration where the servants inherently had the lowliest positions of everyone in attendance. I wonder if they looked around, gazed at the partying crowd, and wished with all their hearts that they could be part of it. Wished that they weren't the "unlucky" servants engaged in the mundane and foolish-looking task of filling stone jars with water. Wished that they could live the "good life" rather than a life that was viewed with disdain. As I consider these details, I am filled with an even greater respect for these servants, because regardless of whatever pain or misunderstanding they may have experienced as a result of their obedience, their response was unaffected—to the brim!

Their example is both encouraging and challenging to me, since I, like the servants, am not currently where I want to be. Or maybe it's just that my chain of expectations seems to be several links short of fulfillment. We all have those "If-I-do-this-then-God-will-do-that" grids of processing that can cause us disappointment or feelings of spiritual inadequacy when things don't work out as we had hoped. Because of times like these, I have had to adjust my understanding of what true servanthood yields.

Just the other night I was strolling the streets of Chicago. I had the evening off during a radio promotional tour, and I simply couldn't resist the rush that accompanies braving city streets at night. (Okay, I was on Michigan Avenue and it was only 5:30.) As I walked I encountered the gamut of city life—everything from taxi drivers giving me unfriendly gestures because I unthinkably tried to cross the street when the sign said "Walk," to a man hand-feeding his dog Gino's pizza, to a disposable-incomed yuppie purchasing at least eight pairs of Diesel pants (which by my estimation would have run him well over one thousand dollars), to the commonplace homeless people. All of this fascinates me—the convergence of rich and poor, sprinkled with the middle class. Perhaps not unlike the group that gathered at the wedding in Cana.

Normally I drink it all in like a milk shake—several entities blended together into one big tasty experience. But this particular night I was cut to the quick by someone who stood out from the crowd: a homeless woman in a wheelchair who was asking for money. For some reason she, out of every other beggar on the street, broke my heart. As I walked past her, I felt a pressing need to do something, to encourage or connect with her in some meaningful way. Yet somehow, at the same time, stopping to talk with her was the last thing I wanted to do. So I kept walking, unsuccessfully trying to quiet my conscience. *Giving her money will only help her in the moment,* I reasoned. *Presenting her with the Four Spiritual Laws isn't engaging enough, not to mention that she's probably heard them so often from street evangelists that she could quote them from memory. Just pray for her, keep walking, and look for discount designer jeans.* To justify my thinking, I made a deal with myself and with God that if I passed her again I would do something. What kind of something, I didn't know.

I shopped around unsuccessfully for a while, and then began heading back on the opposite side of the street. And, of course, as only God could arrange it, this woman had managed to work her way across six lanes of traffic and was now right in my path. *Okay, I have a few dollars. That should suffice.* But I knew God wanted me to offer her something more than money; I knew in my gut that giving her money would only be filling the jar halfway. Shaking off a rising conviction, I placed the money in her hands, breathed the conventional "God bless you," and deeply hoped the money would buy peace for my soul. I thought it would be worth a few bills to get the conviction off my back.

But as I continued walking, I felt no relief. Every step I took away from the woman felt like a step toward some sort of magnetic field that repelled me. I had to go back. After many years of learning to discern God's voice, I knew that my feelings for her weren't springing from garden-variety legalistic guilt, but from the gentle nudge of God's Spirit. So I chose obedience, if somewhat reluctantly.

I turned around and headed back toward her, having no idea what I was going to say. I was just hoping to have some sort of influential exchange. I wanted to offer her Christ in a way that was more definitive than U.S. currency and less impersonal and offensive than shouting scripture from the sidewalk. As I awkwardly approached her—for the third time—it came to me out of the blue: I would ask her if she had eaten dinner.

"Hey again… Just wanted to know if you've had anything to eat tonight."

She politely shrugged with an inquisitive smile. "Not too much."

Ahhh, I'm on to something, I thought. *We'll go to dinner and we'll sit and talk, and at least she'll know that someone cares for her. I'll share about life—nothing too deep, of course—find out a bit about her, and maybe present her with a taste of Jesus Christ. Smitten, she'll inquire with desperate curiosity, "Tell me, what must I do to be saved?"*

It was a noble thought at least. We went into the Subway sandwich shop (her choice). She picked out a turkey sandwich and a Pepsi. I grabbed a salad and water and was up for dessert, but she was uninterested. The cashier began bagging all of our stuff, to which I remarked, "Oh, I think we'll be eating this here."

I turned back to my new acquaintance to make sure this was okay, to which she replied, "Actually, I'd better get that to go."

That really should have tipped me off that perhaps she wasn't as into spending dinner with me as I was with her, but in my zeal to direct the script according to what *I* thought was supposed to happen, none of that registered.

So I walked out of the shop and followed her as she wheeled back to her spot on Michigan Avenue. I figured we would just eat together on the street—no big deal. It never occurred to me that maybe she had asked for her sandwich to go not because she didn't want to eat *in* the restaurant, but because she didn't want to eat *with me*. This reality began seeping into my naive mind when, on our way back, she said in a surprisingly savvy, would-you-please-take-a-hint kind of way, "Weeeeellllll, I'd better take my sandwich and call it a night."

Call it a night! She was dropping me like a bad date! And I

hadn't even "helped" her yet. I had barely had the chance to talk about life and God and how much he loves her.

So I handed over her dinner, left her with a few parting words, then strolled through the streets with the biggest bewildered grin on my face—the kind of grin that says, *Is it just me, or did I just do something I didn't want to do because I thought God told me to do the thing I didn't want to do, and then when I did that thing I really didn't want to do, not only did none of the things happen that I hoped would happen, but I got blown off in the process?*

Because these things puzzle me no end, later that night I sought perspective from one of my favorite people to bounce these kinds of questions off of: my friend Margaret. "Maggie, did I not hear God correctly? I pursued this woman like I was sure God wanted me to, and it didn't seem to end up anywhere. What was the point? Why did God put her on my heart so strongly, all for nothing?"

I won't soon forget Mag's response. "Kelly, we all have our own fantasies of how things are supposed to play out when we choose to obey God. But your responding to God's prompting, your turning back and buying the woman dinner, your following her back to eat with her—*that* was the point! Obedience is an end in itself. It's our own ignorance to think that being of service will yield a particular outcome. We have to leave the results to God."

Maggie was right: Filling the jar to the brim was the point. Period. What God wanted to do with and through me was his part of the story.

I have taken Maggie's words to heart because the life I am currently living at twenty-eight is not what I thought it would be like. I thought my obedience would secure me greater career success and a respectable income and perhaps a husband and children and quicker character changes and smoother relationships...all coated with a sweet, spiritual glaze. But it hasn't quite worked out for me that way. I'm still single and my career is not exactly where I want it and people take their sandwiches to go and sometimes I have to fill up jars with water when everyone really wants wine. But none of this gives me permission to alter my response to God. Just like the servants at the wedding in Cana, I can't allow tough circumstances to be excuses for my giving anything less than to the brim. My own experience testifies to the truth that obeying, serving, and surrendering usually aren't convenient. But could wine be in the making?

This glorious possibility gives a different ring to the words *obedience* and *servanthood.* It affirms the New Testament words, "[God's] commandments are not grievous" (1 John 5:3, KJV). It reminds us that God's heart is tender and loving. He is worthy of all our trust and of every last drop we are willing to give him—not just so that we can receive winelike blessings from him, but so that we can bless the One whom we love with all our hearts. Intimate friendship with God is the true wine.

It's simply speculation, but the servants may have been prompted by a similar desire for intimacy. I am inclined to believe this because turning water into wine was Jesus's first recorded miracle. In light of this fact, how could the servants have ever suspected that their obedience would be blessed the way it was? Up to that point, Jesus had left no trail of miracles for them to put their hopes in, which suggests that they may have been motivated by something other than what they stood to gain. Perhaps this is why they gained so much!

There have been a few occasions, which I pray are becoming more frequent, when I have taken the servants' risk and filled the jars to the brim. Occasions when I have turned everything over to God, with no expectations of getting what I wanted in return. In fairness, I will admit that these times have just about killed me, because when you fill the jars to the brim, no personal reserve remains. If you give everything to God, and things don't turn out as you had hoped, you don't have so much as a sliver left to hang on to—nothing to clutch in your hand while you say to God, "At least you didn't get *this!*" "To the brim" means holding nothing back. To me it's the quintessential picture of what it means to trust Jesus.

Free-Falling

I remember a moment in Nashville when my heart began to reflect the servants' hearts with a bit more purity—a moment when one of my tugs of war with God ceased and the end of the rope I had been clinging to dropped. My fears and my doubts stuck around for a while, but something in my heart had shifted. Of this I am certain.

In April 2000 I had the privilege of being part of an evening of worship at the Ryman Auditorium, a famous historical venue in Nashville. I was asked to sing in a choir composed entirely of recording artists as part of a kickoff event for the annual Gospel Music Association Week. I can't remember the exact song we were singing, but as I stood there on stage, swept up in the fragrance of a thousand praising voices, I remember coming to a defining decision—a decision to release my entire fistful of dreams in one painful but liberating moment to the God who had been tenderly asking for them. It became apparent to me that deeming his glory as more precious than my own meant giving him the freedom to do whatever he wanted with my goals, my music, my career—my life. In short, it meant giving "to the brim." I realized that I really didn't want to hold on to what was ultimately his anyway. He could have it all.

I wish I could report that in the moments following this relinquishment angels swooped down from the ceiling speaking prophetic words laced with promises of success and ministry beyond my wildest dreams. Or that a supernatural peace swept over me, numbing me to all of my past fears and concerns about what God might do with my most valuable wishes—now that he had them. Or that because I had surrendered my plans to God, he promised to give them back to me in short order. But nothing quite like this happened.

Instead, I felt as if I were free-falling off a cliff, unsure whether there was anything below to catch me. Yet there was something more peaceful about the risk of free-falling than there was about clutching what I knew I shouldn't be. Though I didn't necessarily feel safe or that my struggle was resolved, I remember this as one of the most remarkable worship experiences of my life. Worship, not because of great music or well-crafted melodies or an auditorium full of singing people. But worship because it cost me something.

When I recall that night, I can't help but think of Abraham. God instructed him to sacrifice his beloved son, Isaac, and Abraham was poised to obey. As he was on his way, the place of sacrifice looming in the distance, he turned to his servants and said, "Stay here with the donkey while I and the boy go over there. We will worship and then we will come back to you" (Genesis 22:5). I believe that Abraham specifically used the word *worship* here because what he was about to hand over to God was, by far, his greatest treasure. In this act of worship, he was demonstrating his profound love for God.

Similarly, King David, when looking for a place to build an altar to the Lord, insisted on purchasing the altar site even though the owner offered to give David the property as well as oxen for the sacrifice and wood for the fire. David graciously responded with a bold, yet touching expression, "I will not sacrifice to the LORD my God burnt offerings that *cost me nothing*" (2 Samuel 24:24, emphasis added).

Worshiping God is costly. It is not confined to the singing of praise songs or the raising of hands. And it most certainly doesn't

materialize out of Sunday-morning lip service or the empty promises
we make to God in front of those we esteem. It is only when we
hand over to God our most coveted prize, pay a personal price to
serve him, and fill the jars "to the brim" that we will experience
worship in its truest form. Because worship is about obedience and
servanthood. It's about faithfully walking over to the stone jars and
pouring and pouring until there's nothing left to pour. Until all
that we are holding back has been wholly given over. Until our
pitchers are empty, but his are full. Until the last drop has fallen
and we no longer have anything left to hold...but everything left
to gain.

I cannot offer you a cliché ending about how everything has
worked out in my life since I released my career to God. I would
never want to undermine the difficult nature of obedience, surrender, and servanthood by doing such a thing. But I cannot deny that
in the dismantling of some of my dearest dreams and desires, I
have found the heart of God to be amazingly loving. Through the
loss of my first record deal, the disappointment of pouring three
years into a record that was barely released, the humiliation of not
"succeeding" like others around me, the burden of staying afloat
without secure financial backing, the string of seemingly endless
months when the phone didn't ring and there was little work
except for trimming shrubs and mowing a friend's lawn (hardly the
glamorous life I had moved south for), God has been satisfying the
desires of my heart in ways I could never have expected. He knew
that these deep desires could never be gratified by external successes.

He knew I had reached a season in my life when I needed undistracted time to cultivate rich friendships that would sow love and acceptance into my soul—gifts I could never have received while touring away from home. He knew I had deep questions about him that were legitimate and right and needed to be asked—and had I become a public figure during this time, the onslaught of demands would never have allowed these questions to surface, because I would have felt obligated to propagate status-quo responses to keep my ministry "safe" and afloat.

I was initially dismayed when, instead of the successes I was after, God gave me long seasons of alone-time with him. Seasons not necessarily filled with peace and stillness, but with temper tantrums and desperate prayers and wrestling matches that have yielded greater trust on my part. I am beginning to realize that the things I really came to Nashville for were love, relationships, and an honest friendship with God. I thought I would secure these things through a fledgling yet flourishing musical career, but God knew so much better. I couldn't have gotten them on any other path than the one through the valley. I can unequivocally say that I wouldn't change a thing.

Of course, this doesn't mean that I no longer wrestle mightily with the puzzling realities of life or wake up every morning with a compelling desire to pursue the next rung on the career ladder. It just means that I'm quicker to drop my end of the rope, quicker to allow my tug-of-war matches to give way to an intimacy with Jesus that I want more than anything else. This is why the servants at Cana intrigue and challenge my heart so intensely. Because they are the ones Jesus confided in. They are the ones who got to share in a secret that only servants can know.

2

THE SECRET ONLY
THE SERVANTS KNEW

Secrets. They have always been a source of intrigue for me. As a child I liked nothing better than when one of my friends would cup her hand around my ear and whisper, "Shhh, don't tell, *but...*" Secrets were the dividing line on the playground because they had the power to draw stark lines of division or tie strong cords of friendship. They could keep people in or out—there was no in-between. They possessed the ability to be life-giving or life-damaging, depending on which side of the secret you were on. And, of course, few things were worse than having your secret spilled for public consumption by someone who had double-crossed her heart and promised to stick a needle in her eye if ever your secret should slip from her mouth. I suppose we would all be blind if we had held fast to our elementary-school promises.

But as we grow older, we realize that keeping secrets only strengthens our loyalty and resolve. We can still be tempted by that insatiable urge to share them irresponsibly, but we quickly learn that the moment we give in to such urges by divulging another's secret, our desire is never satiated, and the secret that once held such worth is suddenly deflated of its value. Our betrayal is like a pin to a balloon.

One of my best friends is a bit of a leaky faucet when it comes to keeping secrets. She's a sure bet to keep the "big" ones, but anything that is of moderate importance is a real tossup. It took me several months to realize that when she promised not to tell something, what she really meant was that I should be happy to know that she would use her own discretion. This finely tuned "discretion" propelled me into a number of awkward moments that I would rather have avoided. After each violation, we'd go 'round and 'round about the difference between my definition of "don't tell" (which, for some odd reason, meant "don't tell") and hers, which was something more along the lines of "I promise not to tell unless I feel for some reason that I should." We laugh about it now that we've gotten our definitions straightened out. I haven't found my secrets compromised in at least a few months now.

When we were growing up, my siblings and I also had a small rift over this issue of secrets. I have two younger sisters and a younger brother who is the "baby" of the family (I use this term loosely since he is six-foot-three and weighs two hundred pounds). To this day the three of them maintain that my parents consistently left them out of "top-secret" conversations, confiding only in me because I was the oldest. Of course I had no trouble with the fact that my parents entrusted me, exclusively, with certain things; I simply viewed it as a privilege that came with being the firstborn child. After all, it was one of the few perks I had as a firstborn, and I wasn't about to give it up easily.

The tables have been drastically turned now that I am living away from home, however. Megan, Katie, and David collectively remind me that *they* are now the ones who are filling *me* in!

A secret represents so much to me. When someone confides in me, it strengthens the bond between us. It conveys the message that this person considers me trustworthy and that he is willing to place in my possession something that is of great value to him. More often than not, I am far more touched by this gesture than I am by the secret itself; the actual information is secondary to the fact that someone would find me worthy of holding his treasure. To be told a secret is about being chosen, set apart, singled out, because a secret, by its very nature, is something that is not known to everyone. It is for select ears only. A secret is secret only if it is kept.

THE GOD OF SECRETS

Being entrusted with a secret by another human being is an awesome privilege; being entrusted with a secret by God himself is supreme. I believe the latter point has been largely overlooked, especially in our Western culture, as it has been entirely too easy for us to receive general information about God from the spoon of another's hand. We have vast resources available to us concerning our faith and values, which is not inherently bad but can become so when these resources are readily accepted as a substitute for knowing Christ intimately.

Many of us (myself included) have relied too heavily upon the secondhand information we glean from church services, seminars, books, and other Christian resources to define our relationship with Jesus. We fall back upon what our religious community dictates we should believe, ultimately settling for a very impersonal framework that only broadly ministers to our specific needs. Often we are encouraged to fit our uniquely fashioned souls into a one-size-fits-all belief system. As a result, we don't have to work as hard on a personal relationship with God, but I believe it leaves us with a very anemic concept of what it means to be a Christian. Somehow, growing up in a devoutly Christian environment, even I missed the truth that God is not a God of some distant and impersonal religion, but a God of secrets. And, better yet, a revealer of them.

This discovery, at least in part, was unearthed for me by the servants at the wedding in Cana. Not only did they challenge me by their willingness to perform their task with excellence—*to the brim*—but they also confronted me with their humility by bringing water to the master of the banquet when they knew he was expecting wine. When the master took a sip, he tasted something strikingly different from what the servants had drawn and carried to him with their own hands. He tasted a wine more decadent than anything he could have imagined; however, Scripture tells us that he had no idea where it had come from.

As I continued reading I discovered something that began to change my former view of servanthood, which, in all honesty, had represented to me constraint, boredom, and everything distasteful. One of the most poignant lines in the scriptural account came to life for me—the kind of line that, like a dangling thread when slightly tugged upon, unravels a host of treasures and secrets too abundant to be grasped: "The servants who had drawn the water *knew*" (verse 9, emphasis added).

In the midst of honored guests, silk gowns, live music, a bride, a bridegroom, and a master, the lowly servants were the ones who held the sacred knowledge of where this wine had come from! Does it get any more profound than this? There is nothing dry or mundane about this kind of intimate knowledge. There is nothing predictable or dull about the life of a person who walks closely enough to Jesus to be involved in his miraculous and wondrous workings. To know the ins and outs. To see what others have never seen. And, most amazing, to possess divine secrets in such a way that sweetens intimacy with Christ beyond measure.

The servants who had drawn the water knew.

How beautiful to see the value that Jesus placed on these servants who had, on this occasion, become his very hands and feet. They were the extension of his heart, the ones who had carried out his desires. They were not nameless faces, mechanically taking orders like robots. Rather, they were valued people to whom Jesus chose to reveal his secret.

As I contemplate these servants, I cannot help but covet their privileged position, yet my heart is simultaneously pricked with the uncomfortable conviction that servanthood requires so much of us. The servants' job that particular day in Cana was more than likely their job every day. They would probably never hold a coveted position at a grand affair such as a wedding. They might never be honored guests or members of a bridal party or masters of a banquet. They held one of the most humble and lowly positions in life, but in the end they enjoyed something more precious than anyone else in the room: the intimate confidence of the Savior.

In my own life, I am turning a corner in my relationship with God as it relates to waiting on him to reveal his secrets to me. Slowly I am learning the practice of pouring out my heart before him, humbly asking for his whispers and revelations. I have come to this place out of desperation. I can no longer live according to the premise that God resembles a gold mine that has been sifted through and picked over, leaving me only with what someone else has already discovered about him. There has to be more.

I suppose my desperation and my pursuit of "more" stem from many years of consuming a Christian "diet" that was composed mostly of prepackaged fare. Rules, principles, and doctrines were served to me on a regular basis, but in some ways this diet stopped just short of giving me a soul-fulfilling relationship with God. Whenever any question or difficulty arose, I simply searched for the "appropriate" response and plugged it in. God became somewhat unnecessary.

As I have matured in my life and faith, however, I've realized that life does not—will not—fit into a box. Therefore, God is essentially necessary. I need his intimate whisper in my ear to help me discern what to say, whom to say it to, how to respond, and what to accept or reject.

Recently I have found great encouragement and insight from the life of Daniel, who literally staked his life on the fact that, indeed, there *is* more: God shares secrets. Daniel was an unlikely hero who assumed the daunting task of deciphering a king's haunting dreams that had left the best and brightest in the kingdom mystified. With their necks on the line, Daniel was their final hope (see Daniel 2:5). But Daniel was unqualified, ill-equipped. He needed something specific to help him. No previously recorded sermon would do. No spiritual bestseller would be worth pulling from the shelf. Not now. Not even God's written Law would be able to solve this riddle. Daniel needed God himself to speak to him, to share with him the secret. Petitioning God for the interpretation of the dream, Daniel trusted that God had something new to say. That he wouldn't leave Daniel grasping for crumbs at the table of someone else's experience.

Daniel trusted wisely. God revealed to him the meaning of the dream in a vision, prompting a fragrant prayer that has become a favorite of mine: "Blessed be the name of God for ever and ever: for wisdom and might are his.… He revealeth the deep and secret things" (Daniel 2:20,22, KJV). Daniel's experience reminds me that it is not up to me to uncover the secrets as much as it is up to God to reveal them. "No wise man, enchanter, magician or diviner can explain to the king the mystery he has asked about," Daniel said, "but there is a God in heaven who reveals mysteries" (verses 27-28). He knew that honed skills, sharp minds, and even supernatural channeling were not sufficient to crack the king's mystery. He was all too aware that the deep things of God cannot be unearthed, only revealed.

We discover these secrets only when God pulls back the curtain at just the right time, revealing what we otherwise could never have known. They apply directly to our specific hour and need. They bring us face to face with God in the most intimate and transforming way.

Intimate Encounters

Several years ago I was walking the tumultuous and miry road of an ailing relationship. I was literally at my wit's end; my tears exhausted me into sleep each night. No amount of wisdom or personality or talent could remedy the situation. My bag of resources contained no fitting tool—I wielded each one to no avail. The relationship was slipping through my hands like powdery sand that can never be scraped up in the same way again.

I will never forget being awakened one night by my own sadness. I spoke out into the dark silence, breaking the stillness of the air with the words: "God, meet me in my loneliness."

I can't remember specifically what prompted me to open my Bible to the second book of Chronicles, but as I flicked on the light and began to crinkle the pages of Scripture, I came across a verse that cut to the core of my dilemma. The words spoken centuries ago to soldiers facing what appeared to be a losing battle seemed lovingly directed at me in my middle-of-the-night anguish: "This is what the LORD says to you: 'Do not be afraid or discouraged because of this vast army. For the battle is not yours, but God's.... You will not have to fight this battle. Take up your positions; stand firm and see the deliverance the LORD will give you'" (20:15,17).

The Lord was speaking these ancient words to the heart of a girl who was crying out to him on her bed. He was speaking *to me.* He told me not to fight anymore—not to battle for the heart or affections of my friend. He told me to sit still, to trust, and to see his salvation in the midst of a hurtful situation.

A radical shift took place in my soul. I felt a definite release in my spirit and a peace that washed aside my determined strivings to fix whatever I thought I could. I now knew better because the Lord had let me in on something that only he could have known. He had shared with me a secret: This was his battle, not mine.

The insight God granted me that night drastically changed my perspective and dealings with my friend. I held my tongue and waited on God to author the rest of the story. It was not an easy road. My pain and anguish did not vanish with the darkness as morning broke the following day. I still cried and tended my wounds as I had before, but I did so with the fresh knowledge that God was working on my behalf, that he knew my longings and planned to satisfy them, whether through this relationship or another.

As I continue to encounter my own puzzles and obstacles, I find my greatest peace in straining for the whisperings of God. I think back with a holy covetousness to the wedding servants. In a sea of successful people, they held one of the lowliest jobs, yet at the same time, they held the greatest secret anyone could ever know: where true wine can be found. This secret was not something they fought for or breathlessly strove to uncover. They simply showed up. They faithfully upheld their duty. They listened to the voice of Jesus and quietly fulfilled his request. There was nothing for them to uncover; there was simply something for God to reveal. Scripture tells us that the secret things belong to God, but the things that have been revealed belong to us—forever (see Deuteronomy 29:29).

I am not one to keep things this simple, however. My propensity for making the Christian life a matter of figuring out the "formula" for making wine has led me down countless arduous paths—straight into the dead end of myself. The good and relieving news is that I am beginning to loosen my grip on the absurdly misguided and arrogant idea that I am capable of doing anything except handling the water that only Jesus can transform into wine.

WATER IN...WATER OUT

Never have I been more aware of my inability to make the Christian life "work." Growing up in a Christian home, I was blessed with myriad resources that should have ensured a better track record. I was raised in the quintessential version of the "evangelical subculture," and although I was not the most compliant child to emerge from the womb, I did diligently seek to abide by fundamental evangelical virtues. I was certain that, given enough time, most of my rough edges would be filed down and my struggles pounded out. Alas, here I am: unrefined and not nearly where I supposed I would be. Worse yet, not at all where I thought I *should* be.

As far as I understood, I needed only to employ the resources and follow the principles that I had been given, and everything would fall into place accordingly. My list of resources consisted of the usual ingredients for good Christian living: reading my Bible, going to church, praying, choosing my friends wisely, avoiding sin and temptation, making sacrifices, and accepting that I'm on a narrow road that will mostly feel stiflingly snug. I believed that sticking to this formula with earnest effort would guarantee me a victorious and abundant Christian life.

But after years of clinging to a template that has boasted many such promises, I have found myself disillusioned—because my best efforts at executing my list of dos and don'ts has not resulted in the desired outcome. My most noble attempts haven't banished my jealous thoughts or silenced my tongue or settled my anger. I have not been able to still my racing mind, calm my worries, or slay my fears, regardless of how hard I have tried. Adhering to my list has helped me gain a measure of control over my actions, but not over my heart. It has left me with all the answers for winning a theological argument, but it hasn't settled the deeper questions of my soul.

These questions and rumblings manifested themselves even in the loving environment in which I grew up. A Christian environment. One in which my parents loved each other, loved their four children (who weren't always that lovable), and painstakingly laid a godly foundation on which we could build our lives. I'm so grateful for these building blocks because they are the unshakables upon which my faith rests. But they didn't inoculate me or my family members from hardship or sin or things that were grossly unfair. Simply trying to implement all I had been taught was not remotely adequate when it came to handling the riddles and trials of life.

Most disconcerting of all was coming to the realization that I could not change myself by practicing all that I knew. I was—and am—powerless to change my own heart. This startling truth lead me to another realization, a mental cue card that I had been afraid to read aloud: *This whole thing just doesn't work.*

This truth has impressed itself on me at the most surprising moments. For example, I recently flew home after being gone for almost two weeks. After long stints of travel, I usually unwind by checking my voice mail and e-mail as soon as I walk in the door. (This suddenly sounds dysfunctional to me.) Anyhow, both tasks require a working phone line, which, I discovered upon my arrival, was not working. Apparently, the problem was due either to a line in the area being down or, worse yet, some malfunction in my home, which, the Bell South operator politely informed me, my service agreement would not cover. She continued her encouraging monologue, telling me that my service would be restored just as soon as she could dispatch someone, which she guaranteed would happen within the speedy time frame of just four days. This was a problem only because I was expecting it to be fixed somewhere in the neighborhood of four minutes.

I usually don't show it, but this is the kind of stuff that throws me. In fact, I'm overly bugged. I became even more troubled, however, when I realized that my overreaction to small things not working out just the right way—such as missing the tollbooth with my last coin, discovering that my car won't start, or getting a bad grade on a test I diligently studied for—was just a minor reminder of the very major things in my life that weren't "working." These little snafus just confirmed the fact that no matter how valid my efforts, life was not working; Christianity was not working. And that gave rise to my greatest fear: God must not work. At least not for me. No matter how well-intentioned my efforts, I wasn't getting things right.

A PAINFUL DILEMMA

In truth I felt a constant rub between what I thought *should* be happening in my Christian life and what was *actually* happening. Grief, sadness, and even anger at "the system" weighed heavily on my heart. I had been promised that if I did certain things, life would puzzle-piece itself together. Life would "work." But all of my tiny, unresolvable issues reminded me that it simply wasn't so.

The late Watchman Nee wrote in *The Normal Christian Life,*

> At the beginning of our Christian life we are concerned with our doing, not with our being; we are distressed rather by what we have done than by what we are. We think that if only we could rectify certain things we should be good Christians, and we set out therefore to change our actions. But the result is not what we expected. We discover to our dismay that it is something more than just a case of trouble on the outside—that there is in fact more

serious trouble on the inside…. Then we come to
the Lord and say, "Lord, I see it now! Not only
what I have done is wrong; I am wrong."[1]

I spent many years attempting, then failing…attempting and
making slight headway, then failing worse than the time before.
Experience has convinced me that this becomes the case whenever
I try to do "good" in my own strength—when I attempt to give
God what I think he wants, only to discover that I can't do it
because what he wants is something that only he, in his supernatural power, can enable me to do.

I have so many personal examples of this, it's difficult to think
of even one… *Jealousy*. There, it just spontaneously popped out
of me.

Jealousy is something I have always been taught to steer clear
of. If I ever sensed a spark of jealousy ignite in my heart, I would
simply recognize that I was jealous and then try not to be. (You can
give this tactic a whirl if you want, but personally I have found it
to be entirely underwhelming.)

Given my drive to be morally "right," I often took my efforts
to overcome my jealousy a step further by trying to be especially
nice to the person who was the object of my jealousy: I might send
a letter, bring over a gift, or say something nice about her. But this
method proved even more futile than the first, because at the end
of my string of efforts, not only was I still battling my jealousy, I
was also frustrated with repeatedly trying and failing. Like a cherry

sitting on top of an ice-cream sundae, this shameful defeat mocked me from the top of my entire dilemma.

I see now that the problem was—and still is—that I was attempting to reach God's standard by my own means. I thought that *as long as I knew what to do, I could do it.* But now I understand that knowing what to do is only the beginning, because there is nothing I *can* do on my own to meet any of God's standards. "Apart from me you can do nothing," Jesus said (John 15:5).

Of course, in general I can do all kinds of things. But they are "water" things. They are not eternal or supernatural or holy things. "Wine" things, on the other hand, can be accomplished only with divine help. Simply doing all the "right" things, in and of themselves, only leaves me with colored water. It looks authentic from the outside, but when others get close enough to imbibe, they discover that it is tasteless—because my good works and my attempts at righteousness are not of miracle caliber. I need God to actually *transform* my jealous heart. For this to happen, I have had to submit myself to whatever he wanted to do in me, which has sometimes meant allowing him to use the very person I was so jealous of as an instrument of change in my life. I have had to ask myself hard questions such as, Why do I feel so threatened by this person? What does she have that seems more important to me than what God can provide? What am I afraid this person will take away from me?

When I worked through these questions, my jealous twinges eased dramatically. I was no longer dealing with the "problem person"—it was never about that person anyway. It's always about some area of my life that God is trying to get at, an area I keep within my own clutches and out of the reach of his transforming power. As I've released the things God is asking for, I am free to not be jealous because I no longer feel threatened. All is his.

Of course, this is the Cliffs Notes version of several long-winded battles over just *one* of the many issues in my life. The actual pathway to this conclusion was not quick or tidy or succinct, but it did end in a new understanding for me: The transformation of my character is not about *trying harder* to rid myself of jealousy, but about allowing God to do a deeper work in my heart so the root of jealousy can be pulled out. This can never be accomplished through the strength of my life; it can only be accomplished through the weakness of my death...death to myself.

After many years of attempting and then failing in several areas, I find great solace in Paul's angst-ridden lament over doing the things he doesn't want to do, while not doing the things he wants to. "What a wretched man I am!" he cried. "Who will rescue me from this body of death?" (Romans 7:24). If the passage ended right here, I would be grateful that I had at least found an empathetic fellow struggler in Paul, but I would still be just as void of hope and help. So I am ever thankful that the passage continues: "Thanks be to God—through Jesus Christ our Lord!" (verse 25). My hope and healing and the answers lie in the person of Jesus and in his amazing grace.

Liberating Truth

For the majority of my school-age years, I attended private schools that seemed to miss the concept of grace altogether. *Grace* was a word linked only to salvation. As far as I understood, it existed to get me to heaven, but beyond that it was entirely up to me to be good and do the right thing.

I have a litany of memories of those years, but some memories etched themselves deeper into my soul than others. One overcast morning had spread its blanket across the blacktop of the parking lot where I was playing during recess. I believe foursquare was the game of choice that day. Before I knew it, I was pulled face to face with my PE teacher, or maybe it was more like finger to face—her finger to my face. This was not unusual, as I had a nose for sniffing out mischief.

This particular time I was getting into trouble for telling a lie that, incidentally, I never told—not because I was such a good kid, but because lying was the chief of all sins, and I had made a habit of dabbling only in the smaller ones, like talking when I wasn't supposed to, chewing gum on school property, and occasionally being what my mom refers to as "sassy."

I've forgotten what kind of lie I was being accused of, but I will never forget this verbatim quote from my teacher: "I hope you are not telling a lie, Miss Kelly Minter, because you are a pastor's daughter, and pastors' daughters have no business telling lies."

Hmmm... This was very interesting to me. So what kinds of people do have business telling lies? An accountant's daughter? The librarian's son? Perhaps, but definitely *not* the pastor's daughter. Thankfully, my parents never put this kind of pressure on me, nor did they teach such destructive thinking.

My teacher, however, was cultivating a toxic idea that others had already planted in my head, and it flourished for many years to come: "As a pastor's daughter, you represent the very essence of Christianity. It is up to you to show everyone else that Christianity works." In keeping with this theory, an accountant's kid must be good at math, a librarian's child must excel in reading, and so on.

The problem with this idea is the fact that we have all gone astray as wayward sheep and have fallen miserably short of the glory of God. This is the core of the Christian message. So while being great at math and reading might be obtainable, being great at being good never equals being righteous in God's economy. Yes, we are responsible to fill the jars, draw the water, and carry the water; but we are not responsible for making the wine.

At first, wading through this process and coming to these conclusions felt as if I was abandoning my Christianity. But I now see that it is quite the contrary: Recognizing my utter inability to maintain a righteous standard is precisely what is required before I can fully *embrace* my Christianity. In *Mere Christianity*, C. S. Lewis wrote, "Thus, in one sense, the road back to God is a road of moral effort, of trying harder and harder. But in another sense it is not trying that is ever going to bring us home. All this trying leads up to the vital moment at which you turn to God and say, 'You must do this. I can't.'"[2]

We are as incapable of living the so-called Christian life as a handful of lowly servants were incapable of serving wine when all they had was water. It cannot be done. We can wish our water would turn into wine, wave our hands magically across it, and earnestly dream about it happening. But the startling, and ultimately liberating, truth is that we are only capable of drawing water.

I hear this truth resounding in the stories of Scripture—stories that tell us about people like the servants at the wedding in Cana. I am reeled in by this account because it so closely parallels my own experiences and struggles. We remember that the servants filled up the six stone jars "to the brim." But Jesus made another request of them that I find curious: He asked them to "draw some out and take it to the master of the banquet" (John 2:8). The word *it* in this passage is very vague. Is *it* water or is *it* wine?

We are given the life-changing answer in a small phrase we read earlier, "the servants who had drawn the water knew." *Had drawn the water!* These four seemingly inconsequential words ease a tension in my faith that I have long been unable to soothe. At first glance, the phrase may seem like an innocuous slice of information, a mere thread of detail. But the word *water* here is more important to me than almost any other word because it highlights the obvious: The servants didn't draw wine. This piece of information cuts to a desperate part of my soul, because it reflects something I have experienced and struggled with for most of my life as a Christian: the idea that those who pour water in will only be able to draw water out. We should expect nothing more of ourselves; it is the only thing we are capable of doing!

For so long I had it all confused. I was under the false impression that if I did the right things by putting water in, I would assuredly draw wine out. You can imagine the guilt and discouragement I felt with each visit to the proverbial stone jars. After all my striving and effort, I walked away with nothing but common water. But this is no different from what the servants carried with them to the host. Because we are not winemakers, and neither were they! We are simply water fillers, water drawers, and water bearers—and this is stunningly good news for anyone who has ever felt the crippling pressure to be a miracle worker.

The apostle Paul touched on this issue when posing the question to the Galatians, "Does God give you his Spirit and *work miracles* among you because you *observe the law,* or because you *believe* what you heard?" (Galatians 3:5, emphasis added). Miracles do not happen because we are skilled at checking items off the good Christian to-do list; they happen when we are willing to believe in a promise—not a promise that life will necessarily "work out" the way we think it should, but the promise of the person of Jesus Christ.

So, once again I hold up the servants in front of my face and see my own reflection, knowing that in many ways I am them—that I have no more ability to make wine come from water than they did. And more important, that I'm in just as dire need of having it happen. I can empathize with the pressure they must have felt, knowing that a bunch of people expected something of them that deep down they knew they could never provide. I imagine they must have felt that a lot was hinging upon their capacity to serve up wine to a group of demanding guests, just as I have felt that a lot is hinging upon my ability to make the Christian life "work."

I was reminded of this nagging feeling one afternoon while fishing off the shores of North Carolina. I was there celebrating Thanksgiving with friends and one of their families. After being on the road for several weeks, I felt my heart leap for joy when we pulled up to our rented condo that perched right on the water. It overlooked a marina and stone jetty that were calling out our names. The spot looked like a surefire hangout for large, gullible fish. It was perfect by all estimations.

The next morning my friend April and I gathered our gear, shoved our heads into snow hats, and headed to the rocky jetty. She baited her hook with raw shrimp that looked slightly tantalizing to me, while I used a bright pink plastic lure that made me want to bite it off the hook—if I had been a fish, of course. There we were: two good friends; bottled sodas; a crisp, clear winter day; waves splashing against the rocks; seagulls swooping against the backdrop of a blue sky; the Neuse River chock-full of a menagerie of fish; and—not a single bite. Not even a nibble. The most excitement I had that day was a tossup between hooking my lure on a rock and pulling up a sizable tree branch.

As I was standing out there on those rocks, my joints freezing into ice blocks, I wondered why God wouldn't just direct an unassuming fish our way. Just think of how much fun April and I could have had if we had reeled in a "big one" that day. I was just dying to wrestle it onto the rocks as I balanced between two stones over the lapping waves. And the thing is, it would have been such an easy fantasy for God to fulfill. But nothing happened. Only a lonely bobber and a not-so-believable lure skipping along the surface of the water, and a cold, impatient fishing partner (me) ready to head back to couch-potato land and stuff myself with cheese puffs.

This is how I sometimes feel in the pursuit of the living out of my faith. I do everything I know to do. I bait my hook, climb out onto the rocks, try to dodge the wind and the cold, strategically cast my line—and often there's nothing. Silence. Or worse, I get hopelessly hung up and have to cut my losses. I come back empty-handed, or with less than I started out with. This is when I feel the despair: I thought the Christian life was supposed to come together better than this.

But as I contemplate the servants, I realize that it's not up to me to make the Christian life work any more than it was up to the servants to create wine from water. Maybe it has more to do with my being faithful and obedient, as the servants were. Because water in, water out was the sum of their personal efforts—nothing more. This is an incredible relief to me because it reminds me, yet again, that I can do nothing apart from Christ. And that is not only okay, it is the only way this life of faith can be.

As I come to the end of myself, I have increasingly found relief from the guilt and restraint that have kept me bound by a law I could never fully obey. It's been a very traumatic, yet liberating, season for me as I have come face to face with the fact that even on my best days, I cannot make wine.

I don't use the word *traumatic* lightly. It's a scary and crushing thing to try so hard to be a kind person, to hold your tongue and temper, to overcome an addiction, to save an ailing relationship, to have wisdom, to pray fervently, to desire God, to obtain certain blessings, and then to seemingly end up with nothing on the end of your line. I think that if we were honest with ourselves, we would realize how disappointed we all are on some level. Disappointed with our inadequacy and our humanness. Disappointed that our lives are messier than we ever thought possible—or spiritually "legal." Even disappointed in God, that he wouldn't see fit to bolster our efforts a little more.

Just last night I was having one of these moments of disappointment. I was standing out on a dock overlooking a serene creek, waiting for the last remnants of the sun to fade behind the reeds. I was grappling with a certain weakness in my character. Someone had hurt me, and I wanted to handle it with dignity and grace. Instead, I felt only anger and self-pity, and with tears streaming down my cheeks as I looked up at the night sky with all the stars cast over a glorious creation, I couldn't understand why the God who made this magnificence didn't see fit to reach down and deliver me from myself. To fill me with the peace of the Holy Spirit that I had been pleading for day in and day out. I was angry with myself—and with God—that I couldn't "rise above" my hurt, that I couldn't make myself better. I didn't want to be mistrusting or jealous or angry, but I was all those things and felt powerless to change.

The traumatic part is realizing how insufficient I am at the core. Knowing exactly what kind of person I *should* be, but am not. Knowing exactly what I'm *supposed* to do, but cannot. Understanding what my life should look like, yet realizing that my "list" of dos and don'ts does not have the power to get me there.

THE HOPE IN GRACE

I have never been more aware of the truth about myself than I am at this time in my life. I think this is due in part to the fact that I have officially arrived at adulthood and no longer have several years of childhood left to iron out my idiosyncrasies and sinful propensities. I am struck by the fact that I have adhered to a system I thought would deliver me from such things, but instead has kept me tethered to them. My efforts to free myself have been as effective as attempting to beat back the tide with a twig.

In Galatians 5:4, Paul wrote, "You who are trying to be justified by law have been alienated from Christ; you have fallen away from grace." I don't believe Paul was talking about salvation here, but about the grace that empowers us to live for the glory of God in every moment of life. When we strive to accomplish this feat on our own, we render grace insufficient. Of course, accepting grace does not exempt me from responsibility. I do not have the luxury of coasting along on my powerlessness and perceived worthlessness. Grace is not a license to do nothing or, conversely, to indulge my every appetite.

Although it has taken time to work through these issues, it's been imperative for me to eventually circle back to the treasures of biblical wisdom, knowledge, and truth as cornerstone principles by which I must abide. But I know that I can't think of them the way I used to; I can't hold them in my former manner. Now when I think of "the list," the best way I know to describe it is that I am going back to something old in order to find something new. Despite much of the popular religious rhetoric of our day, I cannot depend on the doing of "good" things to grant me a particular outcome. Equally, I cannot assume that my raw abilities will enable me to execute these things well in the first place. I no longer want to force myself to maintain a standard simply because it is the right thing to do. I do not want to assume that my obedience will necessarily secure something I desire or expect. I do not want to forget that it is *God who works in me to accomplish his good will* (see Philippians 2:13) rather than my own sheer and sometimes legalistic efforts. Yet in the middle of wanting to dash away from all of these concepts, I have surprised myself by the ones I have had trouble walking away from.

Recently, while sifting through the legalistic rubble in my mind, I salvaged my weathered list of dos and don'ts, which still includes church attendance, regular Scripture reading, prayer, and other spiritual disciplines. But now this mental list is finding its place in my life as more of an expression of my love for Jesus than a mandate I fulfill in hopes of getting something in return—whether it be approval, favor with God, or a life that "works."

This change in perspective marks the difference between the letter and the Spirit of the Law, legalism and grace, water and wine. What a relief it is to find a welcome camaraderie with the servants at the wedding who understood these truths firsthand. They never abandoned their God-given responsibilities for wild indulgence, nor did they parade around in subtle self-righteousness because they were being obedient. I imagine them having a certain quietness that I long for, a hushed confidence in the One who had asked them to do something they were capable of doing—drawing water—so he could do something he was capable of doing—making wine. This is when our responsibility and Jesus's transforming power touch fingers. It's a beautiful picture of upholding the Law through the means of grace.

A few months ago I was sitting across the table from my friend April. We were grabbing a quick lunch and happened to stumble upon the topic of grace. As I was trying to untangle the idea in my head, I tossed out multiple questions like, Is grace really available for *every* sin, misstep, or wandering? Is it there for all of this, all of the time? Is it always greater than our grievances, or do you think sometimes that it is less?

I will never forget April's poignant words: "Kelly, I don't think grace is more *or* less… It just *is*. Grace just is."

This truth has brought me face to face with having to exchange all of my principles and my neatly wrapped theology for something that "just is." For the *I AM*. So I move toward the stone water jars, pour my commonplace offering into them, and draw out something equally ordinary—not because I can then turn around and demand that God fix something or banish my troubles, and not so I can exchange my jug for a reward or a stamp of approval, but because he *is*. I go, not because it makes sense, but because God has asked me to. And along with his request comes a quiet hope that perhaps one day I will mysteriously walk away bearing wine.

4

BETWEEN DRAWING

AND DELIVERING

I am not a nine-to-five kind of girl. I will work in the middle of the night if it means having the freedom to walk in the park at 1:30 in the afternoon, say, on a Tuesday.

I tend to struggle with the monotony of life. I prefer high highs and low lows to any predictable medium. I enjoy the comfort of a routine, but the routine itself tends to stifle me, and the comfort never feels worth the inevitable loss of what is unpredictable and full of surprise. This mind-set has greatly influenced my work ethic.

I've wiggled out of "regular jobs," so to speak, for most of my life. I've always been a little entrepreneurial that way. As a kid, I mowed lawns, cleaned homes, and watched the neighbors' pets. I also dabbled in my fair share of lemonade stands, even upping the ante by offering fruit smoothies—a secret recipe I had concocted with a neighborhood friend of mine. Growing older only gave way to more adult forms of self-proprietorship—anything to make a buck without having to enter an office.

My sister, Megan, and I are vastly different in this regard. She loves the workplace and everything associated with it: getting up at the same time each morning, wearing business clothes, going to a place where she looks forward to seeing others and being seen. She also has disgustingly perfect handwriting that just cries out to be written down on anything "officey."

Fresh out of college she took a job at a company where she has remained for the past four years—which is three-and-a-half years too long in my mind. She works Monday through Friday in a cubicle, attends company barbeques, has her paycheck directly deposited into her account the second and fourth Friday of every month, and here's what sends me completely over the edge: She wears a badge with her name and picture on it.

That's where I dig a deep trench in the sand. I can't imagine having to wave a card in front of a sensor in order to get into my work pace. Whenever the "badge issue" comes up between Megan and me, I cross my hands around my neck, make wheezing noises, roll my eyes back in my head, and give her the universal choking sign that sends her the message, *I can't imagine being so hemmed in!*

She laughs, then looks at me with pity. Megan happens to view my lifestyle with equal bewilderment. And she has a point. She doesn't get my penchant for toting a guitar around the country, wracking my brain for new melody ideas, and leaving family and friends for just enough money to scrape by on. In a recent conversation Megan made her case: "I would absolutely die if I had to sit in my bedroom in front of my computer, wearing pajamas and trying to think up stories to type into my laptop over a bowl of oatmeal, with no set time to begin or end, all by myself, wondering if any of my work was going to amount to anything, never knowing if I was going to get paid. And you think *my* life is depressing?"

"Well, if you're gonna put it that way..." I began. For one brief second she had me wondering, *Maybe a badge wouldn't be so bad.* Fortunately, I snapped out of it quickly.

I love my freedom. I love what I do and the life I get to live: making art for a living. I thrive on the diversity and challenge of it. The months when I'm not sure how I'm going to make it, as well as those that bring me an overabundance, are precisely what I love about this business. The constant change and extremes energize me. But even with a lifestyle that allows me to be in the studio one week and on tour the next, I still manage to get bored. Or perhaps *bored* is not the right word. Maybe it's more like *stale.* Or, truer still, *doubtful.* I enjoy the constant churning, but underneath the frenetic pace, a haunting voice occasionally makes itself heard over the cacophony, a voice that asks a question I can't seem to answer: *What's it all for?*

What *is* it all for? Another day of work, another day of showing up, another concert, another wedding, another stone jar of water, another order from yet another person: "Fill the jars with water.… Take them to the master of the banquet." The servants had probably been doing this for years. Feast after feast, they served people who were wealthier and higher in status. It was the same rote activity with no shadow of turning.

"Would you care for another hors d'oeuvre?" "May I recommend the salmon puffs?" "May I take your plate?" "Can I get you a refill?"

Day after day. Water in…water out. Routine. Predictable. Monotonous. Mundane. Regimented. What in the world is it all for?

I don't think I'm stretching things by suggesting that this may have been the servants' dilemma, because it seems to me that this is everyone's dilemma: We all go 'round and 'round, attempting to make life work just so we can get up the next day to make it work again. Whether we act on Broadway or deliver newspapers for a living, life doesn't seem to make much sense or have much value without the conviction that God is divinely involved, able and eager to reach down at any moment and turn the everyday stuff of life into something divine, something that counts for eternity, something that is beyond ourselves.

HUMBLE OFFERINGS

A most unsuspecting woman taught me this firsthand. Her name is Sara, and though I didn't know her well before leaving Virginia, I had enough encounters with her to remember her vibrant smile and passionate nature. I remember her as a true "pray-er," someone who would sit in the sanctuary every Monday night and petition God for hours on behalf of the church, the country, and her own heart. I also remember that she didn't drive, but was confined for the most part to her house and lived on a minimal fixed income. But that's pretty much all I knew about her…until she began writing me letters here in Nashville.

It has been such a delight to find her decorative cards among the pile of bills and credit-card offers that have been telling me every week for the past five years that I have been pre-approved for a card—but, perplexingly enough, for a limited time only. About once a month, while hurriedly sifting through such annoyances, I delightfully come across one of Sara's letters. With beautiful handwriting she writes encouraging thoughts and verses, reminding me of how fervently she has been praying for me. But there's something else she never fails to do. On the back of every letter, she neatly tapes a ten-dollar money order. The money comes every month, without fail.

Aware of her difficult financial situation, I sent her a letter thanking her for her generosity to me, but sensitively encouraging her to hang on to the money. I wanted her to know I was in fine shape and didn't want her to feel burdened. A few weeks after I sent the letter, I ran into her on a visit back home. She came up and hugged me joyfully, referring to me as her spiritual daughter in the Lord. But then she got firm with me. "Kelly, when the Lord tells you to give to someone, it is *never* a burden!" She continued to pierce deeper into my heart with her message: "Most people give out of their abundance, but I give out of what I have—which is not much at all. Yet, every time I put that ten dollars in an envelope, I pray that God will multiply it over and over again for you."

Not too long after this conversation, when I found myself in-between tours and, consequently, very tight financially, Sara's ten dollars showed up in my mailbox. After that I received a gift from a relative of five hundred dollars, then a job offer for another five hundred, then a six-hundred-dollar mistake from a company that told me to go ahead and deposit the check, then two unexpected five-hundred-dollar gifts from friends. Two days after that, a church called me to perform, which meant more money coming in that month!

On the way to the airport, I asked my friend Allison if she could swing by the bank. As I was getting my deposit together, I turned to her with my stack of checks and said, "Ali, I'm convinced that all *these* checks are because of *this* check."

I held out the ten-dollar money order. Allison was equally per-suaded. Indeed, God had answered Sara's prayers to multiply her tithe to me. Once she placed her offering in God's hands, ten dol-lars was no longer ten dollars; it became whatever God wanted it to be. And I would rather have ten dollars that God can do some-thing with than thousands that are worth only their face value. Sara is teaching me that water in the hands of God is as good as wine.

Divine Orchestrations

Sara's story is the story of the servants. For them it was the same old, same old, until one day the jars they had filled with water turned into something entirely different. It happened somewhere along the way. Somewhere in the middle of drawing and delivering. They had no idea that their menial task of carrying water would turn into something the world would read about for thousands of years to come. They weren't aware of what had taken place until it had already happened. Until the master began sipping *wine*.

Nothing is said about *when* the water changed. I suppose if we could know these things, we would "show up" only for those specific moments, arranging our lives around the miraculous. But that's what's so great about this story. It's a mystery. The somewhere-in-between housed the miracle. And isn't that the very part many of us wish we could speed up or get around altogether? If only we would be faithful enough to stick around for the humdrum part of the process, perhaps we would witness common water becoming fine wine.

I've been reading about the life of David recently. He is one of my favorites. There is something about the shepherd boy who was chosen to be king, the teenager who slayed a giant, the several-year interval between his anointing and actually sitting on the throne, a thousand side battles, including ups and downs with his children and wives and servants, that spurred more than a hundred psalms that bless and curse, and some that even question God—every part of David's story makes me feel that he is someone with whom I can identify especially well. But in my eagerness to get to his story, I have often passed over the anointing of Saul, probably ignoring him out of my own bias, since his character turns out to be rather disappointing in the end.

But Saul's story is also fascinating—it is a story that should encourage those of us who are weary with the desert wanderings we have to go through for lack of better options. Saul was from the smallest of the twelve tribes of Israel, and according to his own evaluation, his family was the least of all the families that made up the tribe of Benjamin. He was an extraordinary young man who was "without equal among the Israelites" (1 Samuel 9:2), yet he still arose from humble beginnings. This fact reminds me that God often chooses the most common vessels to accomplish his will and reveal his glory.

The curtain is raised shortly after Saul's father had—of all things—lost a number of donkeys. To remedy the loss, he sent his son and a servant on a journey to find them. (It doesn't get much more insignificant or mundane than going on a scavenger hunt for wayward jackasses!) After a few days of searching in vain, Saul wanted to turn around and go back home. But his lowly companion, his father's servant, suggested that they seek counsel from a well-known prophet, Samuel, who lived in the area.

Before Saul even had a chance to go look for Samuel, he discovered that the prophet was heading toward him. What Saul didn't know was that the Lord had already informed Samuel that Saul was coming, and that when he arrived, Samuel was to anoint him king over Israel.

This whole turn of events hits me really funny. Saul was out searching for his father's lost donkeys when he met up with one of the greatest prophets of the Old Testament, who then anointed him king and assured him that his donkeys had already made their way safely home. Clearly, Saul thought he was taking a journey for one reason alone—to lasso his father's donkeys—only to find out that he himself had been lassoed by God for something entirely different: to receive a crown. Who knew life could be so bizarre?

While meditating on the significance of this account in 1 Samuel 9–10, I honed in on a verse containing a single word on which the entire irony of this story seems to hang. "About this time tomorrow I will *send* you a man from the land of Benjamin. Anoint him leader over my people Israel; he will deliver my people from the hand of the Philistines" (1 Samuel 9:16, emphasis added).

Send. God had sent Saul directly to his destiny! From an earthly perspective, Saul was just a young man searching in vain for his father's donkeys. But in the mind of God, he was on a venture that would ultimately make him royalty. Saul had been *sent.* His meeting with Samuel was a divinely orchestrated encounter. Saul thought he was looking for donkeys, when God had actually sent him to be anointed king. The servants thought they were carrying water, when God had really sent them to deliver wine.

This is profound. Yet it is as simple as the stuff of life. It is as

simple as being obedient. As serving. As sitting with the next-door
neighbor to whom your heart is drawn. As making time for a hurting friend. As writing a song when you would rather write a gro-
cery list—or the other way around. As simple as nursing your
newborn or fixing dinner for your family. As sending ten dollars to
someone. As looking for lost donkeys. As being faithful. Faithfully
obedient to Christ in the daily grind, and ultimately finding that
when you thought you were simply asking the not-so-lovely person over for dinner, or giving an anonymous gift, or just going
about your daily duties to the best of your ability, you were really
being sent—by God.

The Miraculous in the Mundane

The fact that God indeed works this way renews my hope. We all
have areas in our lives that cause us weariness; times when we aren't
sure if we're making a difference, and we wonder if we would be
better off doing something else—or doing nothing at all. I deal
with this when I'm out on the road singing. Or when I am at home
writing. *Does anyone hear me? Is anyone moved? Others do this so
much better than I.*

Several years ago, somewhere in the early stages of my singing
career, I had a memorable concert for mostly forgettable reasons:
Hardly anyone was there. It would be hard for me to count the
number of times—especially back then—when I showed up for
performances only to find so few people in the "crowd" that it

WATER INTO WINE

66

didn't meet the definition of the word. These audiences most often resembled small gatherings, like the number of people you invite over to play a round of cards, specifically solitaire.

A few years ago I was slated to perform at an annual festival in my hometown of Reston, Virginia. It's not a huge city, but the festival commands a fairly decent attendance amidst funnel cakes, fresh lemonade, and local talent. The promoter of the event was overly enthused to have me and had gotten the grossly inaccurate impression that since I had done some recording in Nashville, I was a bona fide household name. For some reason he was convinced that the majority of people in the progressively liberal town of Reston would appreciate overt Christian songs sung over the strums of an acoustic guitar. Never mind the fact that even my next-door neighbors barely knew my name, much less anyone else in Reston.

Though I could tell that this promoter was a tad too zealous, I had no idea how far he would run with his misperceptions. But I soon found out in a most disconcerting way. I was on my way to a friend's house when suddenly I noticed something profoundly horrifying hanging from one of our busiest overpasses. It was a bigger-than-life banner heralding the name **KELLY MINTER** in bright, bold letters and welcoming me to the festival as Reston's *special* guest. I was doomed. It was a setup. Failure was imminent.

On the morning of the festival, I showed up at the stage, though I have to use this word loosely. It could more accurately be described as a piece of wood on stilts, covered by a circus tent. The act before me was a children's interpretive dance group of sorts that was really a large gathering of eight-year-olds flailing around in chaotic directions and wearing handmade costumes that didn't match. They were dancing to musical tracks resonating from someone's boom box via a twenty-dollar microphone. It was horrid— but at least there was an audience, I kept telling myself.

An audience, yes. But one that, unfortunately, was comprised primarily of the parents of these darling third-graders. This was bad news. As soon as the event was over, the audience dispersed faster than Olympic runners out of their starting blocks. I looked over the vast parking lot and wondered if asphalt was a connoisseur of my music. After my first song, I heard a few claps coming from a fairly tall man in a ball cap who was standing slightly to the left of the stage. As I strained my eyes, I noticed that he looked strikingly familiar and might even be my dad. Next to him stood my mom, sporting a pair of big black sunglasses and a proud, half-moon smile that stretched from ear to ear. Fortunately a handful of other attendees were there who did not happen to fall in my bloodline—people such as my fourth-grade Sunday-school teacher, my best friend from high school, and some kids for whom I used to baby-sit. Bored, my siblings were off sampling ice-cream flavors and caramel apples, though when I cross-examined them later they claimed to have been within earshot the whole time.

These are precisely the moments when I wonder what it's all for. I may be singing about the love or the sovereignty or the beauty of God, but I'm thinking with dismay, *This is such a waste. Why am*

I doing this? This makes no difference. Then, to my continual amazement, in almost every one of these situations someone will come up and tell me that something I sang about, or happened to say off-the-cuff, was the very thing she needed to hear, or that I met him in a unique and specific way in his life. And those are only the people who choose to share with me.

I understand. I have heard a great many speakers and singers over the years who have touched and blessed me immeasurably but who will never know their influence upon my life because I have never had a chance to tell them. Perhaps while God was using them to deeply minister to me, they were worried about their sick child at home or had just had a major fight with their spouse. Or maybe they felt detached from everything they were saying, wondering if they even believed it themselves. Perhaps they felt, as I so often do, like nothing of value was happening.

But it's the mundane moments you never know about. The hyped-up ones seem to be a sort of end in themselves, as if the exhilaration itself is the prize. But the "normal" moments are the ones you really have to consider. The ones in which nothing seems to be happening at all. Yet these are the times when water could be turning into wine. Or donkeys could be lost while a king was being found. A moment when you thought you were following something only to discover that you were actually being sent.

We can never know. Because the miracle happens somewhere between the drawing and the delivering. Between the seeking and the finding. Between the old and the new. It's all part of the process of being faithful, and it's up to God to reach down and turn the mundane into the divine, the ordinary into the miraculous, the routine into the extraordinary. It's up to us to be faithful. As faithful as humans can ever be.

In my experience, being human is the hard part, because it requires waiting on God to accomplish what I cannot, which is often a struggle. Fortunately I'm not the only person who has ever felt this way. Paul wrote this encouraging reminder to the early Christians in Galatia: "The one who sows to please his sinful nature, from that nature will reap destruction; the one who sows to please the Spirit, from the Spirit will reap eternal life. Let us not become weary in doing good, for at the proper time we will reap a harvest if we do not give up" (Galatians 6:8-9).

5

THROUGH WAIT
AND STRUGGLE

I'm on a plane right now heading cross-country, and, of course, every seat is full—but I will only play so far on your sympathies because I am somewhat pleasantly seated on the aisle. However, two desperately unhappy toddlers—one who is two rows in front of me and the other who is two rows back—are making their misery audibly known to the point where the man in my row by the window is threatening a second Bloody Mary, and the woman beside me is drowning out the noise by losing herself in pop-culture magazines. I, on the other hand, am desperately praying for peace and patience but am growing more irritated with each heightened cry. The woman and man beside me appear fully helped by their means of relief, while I...am very much not.

This is a trivial thing, I realize—figuring out why my spirituality doesn't help me endure a trying airplane ride like the other passengers' drugs of choice. But on a much deeper level, I wonder about the same things when it comes to the bigger questions of life. Where is the help? Where is the relief? While many people are escaping their sorrows through illicit sex and wild partying, or by grasping for money through deceit or workaholism, or even by focusing on seemingly innocent things like nice homes or new furniture, I am often envious—not of their lifestyles, but of their freedom to anesthetize some of the feelings I have to deal with raw.

Sometimes I wish God would show up for me like an effective anesthetic, and that I could occasionally "check out" completely. But I realize that a waiting period is required for spiritual transformation. And we have to go through this waiting period fully alive, with all of our senses keen and functioning. It wouldn't be wise to reach, metaphorically speaking, for a second Bloody Mary or a *Star* magazine, simply because it would dull us to the point where we would miss what we're here for. Maybe this is why God's Word reminds us that at the "proper time" we will reap the good seed we've sown (Galatians 6:9). There *will* be a harvest—if we don't give up during the wait and the struggle.

I wonder how many days or years the servants in Cana served before the water became wine. I wonder if they envied all the pleasure that everyone else seemed to be engaged in—the eating, the drinking, and the dancing—while they went about their ignoble tasks. Did they tire? Did they become weary in the doing? Did they ever feel shamed or hopeless or full of despair? I wonder if things changed for them after not only witnessing the miracle in Cana but actually participating in it. I wonder…

I wonder, because I am hoping for divine metamorphosis in my own life. I am praying that all of the struggles and the uphill battles will eventually turn into something worthwhile. Perhaps they already are, even though I can't see it. But such transformation comes only with patience and perseverance and long-suffering.

Speaking of such things reminds me of Abraham. God had promised him that he would be the father of many nations, that his seed would become more numerous than grains of sand (see Genesis 22:17). But it would take one offspring to create billions. And in a monumental moment in history, God finally promised Abraham that one—a son (see Genesis 15:4-5). Interestingly, the first verse of the next chapter says, "Now Sarai, Abram's wife, had borne him *no children*" (16:1, emphasis added).

Abraham was faced with the ultimate contradiction: miraculous possibility versus mundane reality. Like a scene in a movie, there is the glorious picture of the almighty God promising the aging Abraham a son, then an abrupt cut to scenes of his barren, elderly wife, Sarah. God promised a son, but no children came. At least not for a long time.

God's promises never fail, and they are never given flippantly or without guarantee. But sometimes the spans of time between the promise and the fulfillment of the promise seem unbearable, tempting us to err as Abraham and Sarah did—by attempting to fulfill the promise in our own way. "The LORD has kept me from having children," Sarah said to her husband. "Go, sleep with my maidservant; perhaps I can build a family through her. Abram agreed to what Sarai said" (16:2).

It was the logical thing to do, really. I mean, what else *could* they do? Wait patiently in faith for a miracle? I'm afraid I wouldn't have reacted any differently, as I am well versed in "helping" God when my trust is feeble. I have great faith when it comes to things that don't directly affect me, but when it comes to my own life and plans and the promises God has made to me, I feel the pressing need to lend my assistance. I may acknowledge that he's entirely capable of handling these things on his own, but I'm afraid he won't choose to do what I am hoping, or in the way I am hoping… so I offer him my services.

Abraham and Sarah offered God their services—actually, the maidservant, Hagar, was recruited to offer them—and as a result, Abraham got a son—Ishmael. But this was not the son God had intended to be the father of many nations. That son was Isaac, who didn't arrive on the scene until at least fourteen years after God had made his covenant with the infertile couple.

In a day and culture where waiting more than a few seconds for something to come out of the microwave is an inconvenience, I find that the virtue of patience is not something I have particularly refined. Like Sarah and Abraham, I have asserted myself on so many occasions, trying to push things through by my own hand, forcing the fulfillment of God's promises—but only to my detriment. I have created Ishmaels, who are still running around causing me great heartache and strife, simply because I have been anxious, and couldn't wait, and wasn't sure if God would really come through as he promised. How painful it can be to wait on God; but how much more painful to bridge the gap between promise and fulfillment with my own forceful will, creating confusion and unrest on every side.

ON THE WAY TO THE PROMISED LAND

A few weeks ago I gave a performance here in town for several of the sales representatives of the company that owns my record label. I attended a reception afterward where artists had the opportunity to meet those who diligently sell their records to the stores. As I was sipping punch and shaking hands and trying not to spill anything on my shirt, a little girl unexpectedly latched on to my leg while I was conversing with one of the salespeople. I stroked her head while I wrapped up my conversation, and then I knelt down and asked what her name was and if she had had a good time at the concert. I told her how pretty she was, and by that time, I had pretty much gone through my bag of tricks.

As she responded to my questions in little-girl fashion, I noticed a taller figure standing behind her, whom I correctly assumed to be her mother. She told me that her daughter was dying to know how long I had been playing the guitar because she was interested in it herself. Without thinking too intently, I casually answered, "Eight years." Now there's no way to overdescribe this next part, except to say that the little girl's mouth dropped wide open and her eyes bugged out of her head like some sort of cartoon character's, and she stared at me as if I had just delivered the most staggering, if not depressing, news ever to come her way.

"EIGHT YEARS!" she exclaimed.

I looked up at her mother for a bit of clarification, wondering why all the shock and facial contortions. Her mother smiled at me and offered a very helpful explanation: "She's only six."

I had been playing the guitar two years longer than she had even been alive, so I understood her horror. Eight years is a really, really, *extra-really* long time when you're only six. Comprehending this, I grabbed her cute little arm at one of the creases and, staying right at her eye level, I assured her that she could still start right now and that it wouldn't take eight years for her to be able to play. Seemingly satisfied with my remarks, she waved good-bye and trotted away, leaving me with a fresh perspective: God has asked me to wait during times of preparation for what has seemed to me like eight years to a six-year-old heart.

Two-and-a-half years ago I received a letter in the mail with Isaiah 43:2 written on it: "When you pass through the waters, I will be with you; and when you pass through the rivers, they will not sweep over you. When you walk through the fire, you will not be burned; the flames will not set you ablaze."

A few days before, I had gone through a Bible study on the same verse. Then another note arrived from a different friend who didn't know the first friend, and the very same verse was written on it. Next I heard a sermon in which the verse was referenced.

Within the span of a couple weeks, I had been inundated with a Scripture verse that I had never really given much attention to. I couldn't deny that God was speaking to me. Contrary to the flavor of the passage, however, my life had been going along fairly smoothly, so I wasn't sure what God was trying to tell me. Since nothing like this had ever happened to me before, I decided to journal the many ways this verse had come to me.

I didn't think much about it until months later. Until my life started to unravel one piece at a time. Until I was scraping by financially, and went through some dramatic friendship changes, and lost my record deal, and thought I was losing my identity. Until it seemed that God had forsaken me; until I felt the heat of a fire that was threatening to consume me and was up to my neck in a river that was threatening to drown me. Then, suddenly, I remembered God's words to me.

I rifled back to Isaiah and considered how the verse related to me personally. God seemed to be reassuring me that no part of this frightening experience had escaped his notice. He knew what I was heading into, and he hadn't forsaken me; to the contrary, he was protecting me. As I looked at this passage, I viewed it with new eyes, noticing something I had not recognized before: *through* the waters, *through* the rivers, *through* the fire. Everything was about the going "through" an experience. There would be no going around or under or on top of—or any other way of bypassing it. I

was going to have to taste and feel and touch and breathe the landscape to the point where I thought that the fire would scorch my
skin and the waters would cover my head.

Although I think I might be seeing shafts of light at the end of
the tunnel now (I pray I'm not just hallucinating), I am still somewhere in the middle. I don't know how I am going to pay next
month's bills, or if I will ever not crawl into bed alone at night, or
if my music will get heard this time around, or if the deepest parts
of me will be understood, or if the sometimes agonizing questions
I have about God will ever be answered. For whatever reasons, the
Lord has not yet allowed me to wiggle out of this narrow passage.
I am well acquainted with a new depth of pain, and a dying to self,
and growth in areas in which I didn't want to stretch. The French
mystic Madame Guyon said in one of her letters to a friend,
"God designs to bring His children, naturally rebellious, *through*
the desert of crucifixions—*through* the temptations in the wilderness, into the Promised Land" (emphasis added).

The one redeeming thing about the word *through* is that it
inherently implies another side—a spiritual Promised Land in our
case. *To go through* means passing between something and arriving
on the other side. It is impossible to say you have gone through
something if you end up somewhere in the middle. The word
through also entails movement: You cannot "go through" while
remaining stationary.

God has promised me in Isaiah 43:2 that, indeed, he will take
me through, though it has often felt like the death of me. As bleak

as the dead of winter. But even winter must eventually succumb to spring; it is one of the most redeeming pictures we have in nature.

TRANSFORMATIONS

Growing up near Washington, D.C., I experienced my fair share of icy winters, blizzards, subzero temperatures, and mornings when the engine of my impressive Dodge Omni was frozen solid. Nashville winters are a breeze in comparison, so the fact that winter has spoken to me so poignantly down here has been quite a surprise.

Some of the most glorious parks I have ever walked through are within ten minutes of my home. Even in winter I can't get enough of tossing sticks into the creek for Max to retrieve, wandering through the dense growth of trees, feeling my calf muscles strain as they propel me up the hills, and most of all, conversing with friends about whatever life means to us in that moment. But something else kept striking me internally during that winter of 2002: the barrenness that imbued the park.

I found the winter landscape to be a mirror image of what was going on in my soul: a persistent, bone-aching chill. A barrenness that left me feeling cold and dead and hopeless. Nature's decay struck me deeply as it, too, seemed void of any promise of life. There were no leaves on the trees, just desolate branches, stripped bare, a flat gray against overcast skies and steel water. If I hadn't known better, I would have emphatically deemed that this was the end of the tree's life span, that no hope for new growth remained.

Never would I have ventured to believe that this scene of death was the precursor to life. To spring.

As I walked through the park's seeming breach of promise, a question kept cycling through my mind: *How will change, or life, or growth, or color ever come from* this? I couldn't help asking the same question as I assessed the condition of my own heart and the trying circumstances of my life. I was tempted to strike a gavel in my mind and declare my current sufferings hopeless. But there was a promise in nature and in Scripture that I knew I had to take hold of in a brand-new way: "Whoever loses his life for my sake will find it" (Matthew 10:39).

I think it was around March when I began to stumble upon this life. I had ventured out to the park with a visiting friend from high school, when I became uncharacteristically fascinated by the most peculiar things on the ends of the branches. "Kathy!" I cried. "Come look at these!" As I gently held these tiny outgrowths between my thumb and forefinger, I was overcome with joy and a freeing sense of relief that perhaps this whole awful season of death was transforming before my very eyes.

"Yes, Kelly," Kathy said. "Haven't you ever seen these before? They're called *buds*. We learned about them in biology." (Incidentally, I knew what they were; I just had never appreciated them before.)

As we moseyed down the trail together, it hit me: "Kath, I don't think I've ever *really* noticed spring because I don't think I've ever *really* noticed winter."

I think we have to appreciate death before we can truly appreciate life. In *Self-Abandonment to Divine Providence,* Jean-Pierre de Caussade wrote, "By the same stroke God kills and gives life, but the keener the pains of death, the more intensely does life flow into the soul." Mysteriously, the death of winter is the preparation for the life of spring. But it all takes time. And as my little six-year-old friend reminded me, time can seem like an eternity, especially when God is making incisions into our "self-life."

Then again, time is also frightfully short. I was reminded of this last year when I went back to Virginia for my ten-year high-school reunion. I happened to have a concert in the area and simply couldn't justify passing up the opportunity to go. Assuming that the few friends I still kept up with would be joining me, I registered for a reunion I never thought I'd attend. After all, I wasn't one of those who made especially meaningful attachments to the high-school experience; in fact, school in general was never really my thing. I sort of tolerated it, seeing it as one of those necessary evils like flossing or making your bed in the morning—you just have to do it.

Yet I couldn't seem to quiet the nagging "something" that kept tugging on me to go…maybe to make peace with my high-school experience or to find something redemptive about those four painfully awkward years. Or maybe just because the evening was hanging out there, and I was curious. I'm not sure. I just knew that I felt very strongly about following that determined inner voice… until I called my two best friends from high school and found out they couldn't attend. That bit of information immediately melted my resolve. *No way am I going by myself,* I thought. *I'll eat the ticket and go out for Mexican with my family. Done.* I felt better already.

Except that I didn't really feel better. I felt wimpy and insecure and started having troubling thoughts about passing up the night. *If I don't go, I will probably miss something that I really need to be there for, like meeting my husband or getting a big career break or something monumental that I won't get if I don't go—all because I had a moment of weakness and made a life-altering decision to go have chips and salsa and a bean burrito instead.*

I was panicking, until it finally dawned on me that the whole purpose of the ten years after high school is to mature you so you *can* do things like go back to your reunion by yourself. I mean, if I couldn't manage that, then what in the world had the decade been for? It's as if I was still afraid to walk into the school cafeteria, wondering where I was going to sit, embarrassed that my mom packed my lunch when all my friends were buying. Why did I go through all the struggle and growth of the past ten years if I was still too afraid to show up alone?

So I went out of principle. And it was fun. And I was fine. And I didn't meet anyone who remotely resembled the kind of person I thought could be my husband, nor did I get anything close to a career break or stumble across anything life changing. But at least I noticed something that made me think: The smokers still smoked; they just didn't have to hide in the bathrooms to do it.

The jocks were still pretty athletic; they just had less hair and more weight. The "bad" kids were still bad, though they were more refined at it. The smart people were, lo and behold, still smart: accountants, bankers, lawyers, professors. And—I say this without any intention of sounding cruel—the not-so-cool people were still not-so-cool, though they didn't seem to care a bit about what anyone else thought. I was jealous of them.

Everything had changed, but in reality, nothing had changed. Appearances were different, and lifestyles had morphed with the addition of spouses and children and careers. But mostly, my classmates were just *more* of whatever they had been ten years before. They were further down and deeper into whatever had barely surfaced while we were all in high school together.

I left the party late that night and retraced the roads I used to drive from school to my house. In a poignant moment of reminiscence, I realized that an entire decade had gone by. Just like that. Done. Over. In some ways high school seemed like another lifetime, but in other ways it seemed like only last week when I was at basketball practice, straining to touch my toes in a circle of teammates.

What have I done with the last ten years? I pondered. For eight of them I had played the guitar. I had lived in Nashville for two and a half of them. I had signed a record deal and lost it and signed another one. I had toured the country on the coattails of my music. I had made some incredible friends. I hadn't made much money—still working on that one! But what had my heart done in that time? I guess that's the real question.

Not to make generalizations, but if other people were simply more of what they were ten years ago, I had to ask myself, *Am I more of what I was? Is my heart more united to Christ's? Am I deeper into my spiritual journey? Have I had more "to the brim" experiences? Am I depending less on human arms and more on the invisible but sustaining embrace of God? Am I more of a servant? Do I know more of God's secrets? Have I witnessed more water being turned into wine?*

Those are the important questions, I think. And the answers lie in my willingness to walk *through* the places God is taking me regardless of the fire, in spite of the flood—all the while remembering that Abraham and Sarah waited for Isaac; winter waits for spring; the servants waited for wine. A wine that turned out to be far finer than the usual party fare. In fact, it was the *best* wine around.

6

SERVING THE BEST WINE

It seems that the master of the banquet knew nothing about where the wine had come from, but he did know one thing: He had tasted the finest. His taste buds prompted him to say to the bridegroom: "Everyone brings out the choice wine first and then the cheaper wine after the guests have had too much to drink; but you have saved the best till now" (John 2:10).

I'm not certain why Jesus decided to make the *best* wine when he performed his miracle. Maybe the better question is, Why not? Perhaps this miracle was intended to prove his great power or demonstrate that when Jesus does something, he does it with excellence. I don't know how a Bible scholar would exegete this verse, but I'm certain of one thing: The people *wanted* his wine.

At this stage in American history, it is no secret that Christianity is not the most popular of religious alternatives. American pop culture often makes Christians, especially evangelicals, the butt of its jokes. People offer a disrespectful but telling commentary on how Christians often come across. I think it is fair to say that the world in general is not making a beeline to the table we have set. People are not lining up in droves at our doorstep. They're not thirsty for the wine we're serving.

Many Christians would argue that the world rejects our wine because our beliefs bring conviction, and the darkness hates to be exposed to the light. Others argue that people would simply prefer not to be hemmed in by the parameters of Christianity; they want to live their lives by their own standards, not by the absolutes that such a belief system would impose upon them.

I won't deny that these factors add fuel to the heat Christians take from American society. The teachings of Jesus were not widely popular in his day either. Many people hated him and his disciples and hardened their hearts in exchange for the freedom to do as they pleased. We are also reminded in Scripture that we can expect to suffer for our beliefs. After all, Christianity does not appeal to the lusts of the flesh or the pride of life, two fundamental building blocks of our world system.

These facts, however, are not what cause me the dismay with which I frequently wrestle. They are givens that we know already exist. But they don't explain all the *other* reasons why Christianity is mocked in some circles and, more tragically, why Christians as a whole are not always well regarded.

To say you are a Christian in contemporary American society is to say something that too often bounces off the calloused ears of those who not only think they know what being a Christian means but also want nothing to do with it. In his book *The Divine Conspiracy*, Dallas Willard says,

> My hope is to gain a fresh hearing for Jesus, especially among those who believe they already understand him. In his case, quite frankly, presumed familiarity has led to unfamiliarity, unfamiliarity has led to contempt, and contempt has led to profound ignorance.[1]

I fear that gaining a fresh hearing for Jesus, and essentially for Christianity, is a daunting task because too many of us have skewed his reputation. Dallas Willard is precise in his assessment. As a whole, we have not lived very authentically and have often represented Jesus in ways that must desperately grieve him. We have too often reduced the glory of the gospel to bumper stickers, condemning slogans on T-shirts, and awkward quotes on church billboards. We have unthoughtfully pushed verses or tracts on those who have needed our time, love, and attention more than a quick overview of our beliefs. And we have demanded that people clean up their lives *before* we introduce them to the boundless love of Jesus.

When pondering the water-into-wine miracle, I am pierced by a key question: What kind of wine am I serving? I desperately long to offer something with a rich bouquet, something authentic that the world desires but too often cannot find at church or in other Christian circles.

CHEAP-WINE CHRISTIANITY

Moving from Washington, D.C., to the buckle of the south's Bible Belt has been an interesting transition for me. Besides the accents, overt friendliness, and noticeably slower pace, I have discovered something I have never seen before: church signs. I'm not talking about signs that display informative details like the name of the church and the pastor, and the times of the services. I'm talking about signs that rotate slogans on a weekly basis.

I happen to live on a street that boasts more than ten churches (I'm serious), so I have been forced to get accustomed to this sight. Just yesterday, on my way to a meeting, I drove by a sign that said, "The Cross: the ultimate power tool." A few weeks ago I noticed another sign that read, "Caution: Overexposure to the Son may prevent burning." Or my favorite on the offense list, "Your reservation is for eternity—will it be smoking or non?" It is difficult for me to type these phrases without experiencing that nervous embarrassment you feel while watching someone on stage struggle through a comedy routine that isn't remotely funny. Right now I am squirming at my desk.

I don't in any way mean to come off as superior or condescending, but I think there is something fundamentally wrong with this type of "Christian" communication. I realize that God is capable of using absolutely anything to draw people to himself, but if I were someone who was considering the Christian faith and happened to drive by one of these signs, I can't imagine giving a second thought to attending on a Sunday morning. How can we relegate the profound message of the Cross to a power tool or make light of things as serious as our eternal destiny? I'm afraid this church-sign phenomenon is merely an isolated example of how the rich wine of our faith has been cheapened, making it distasteful and of little value to those who are searching for meaning in life.

I recently pulled out of New Orleans after visiting a Christian radio station in the city. I had a riveting discussion over dinner with Libby, the station's music director, who introduced me to some fresh thoughts on this topic. (She also introduced me to newly important staples: beignets—similar to funnel cakes, but with more class.) We mostly asked each other rhetorical questions, such as, Is Christian music having an impact on the city of New Orleans? Are we only servicing ourselves? Are we so separated from the culture that we no longer have influence?

As we continued our discussion late into the night, we walked to our car, maneuvering through the highly intoxicated, the homeless, and those who had turned rickety card tables into mystical establishments and promised to tell your future. Tarot cards and palm reading met, oddly enough, in front of a magnificent cathedral.

Something seemed desperately amiss. I couldn't help but think how irrelevant I felt as a follower of Jesus. How would these people ever be reached by the gospel? Certainly not by beating my conservative drum while marching around waving picket signs or preaching condemnation on their street corner. I wasn't very sure it would happen through Christian music either. These people didn't need to hear about the issues I stood for; that would only provoke a futile fight between two unbending belief systems. Neither did they need to be converted to my principles or my concept of morality. They needed *Jesus*. Everything else he deemed important would follow.

I think we (myself included) have done the world a great disservice by making our Christianity about issues—about everything from fighting abortion to homosexuality to prayer in school; deliberating over drinking alcohol versus not drinking, homeschooling versus public school versus private school; dating versus courting; antidepressants versus spiritual intervention; Republican versus Democrat; Christian music versus secular; and so on and so on. We seem to have stockpiled hundreds of issues that threaten to obscure the reasons why we are Christians in the first place. We have dedicated books and radio shows and entire ministries to individual topics that we deem critical. But what about Jesus? Where is he in the midst of our issues? I am not pointing fingers; I simply want to express how much I miss seeing the person of Christ in contemporary American Christianity.

That evening as I made my way past the fortune-tellers and the physically and spiritually needy, I couldn't quiet my troubling thoughts. It became increasingly clear to me that "issue" Christianity would never reach these people. It didn't remotely matter whether or not I believed that Christian school is the only suitable option, or that smoking a pipe is a stumbling block, or that taking antidepressants is biblical. Only Christ would matter to these people. And only he has the power to win hearts and set spirits free. But it all begins with the wine we are serving. I can't imagine non-Christians sipping from our chalices of morality and values—much less our angry soliloquies—without first tasting the love of Jesus.

THE RELEVANCE OF JESUS

I have a friend, Eric, with whom I have been very close since childhood. He was raised in the same Christian environment I was, but thus far he's decided to reject Christianity and its God. The deliberate lifestyle choices Eric and I have made over the years have caused us to drift further and further apart. Eric says he no longer believes in God. He doesn't claim to hold to any moral standard, and he strongly rails against the Christian faith. I, on the other hand, have based my music, writings, career, and, more important, my day-to-day living on what I understand to be the call of Jesus Christ. Though I understand some of what has driven Eric's personal decisions, we are like two sides of a triangle that lean in entirely different directions but remain connected by a point: our love for each other.

The two of us are planning to work together on a secular music score in the future and look forward to mingling our creative abilities. Eager to get working on the details, Eric called me late one evening to discuss the project. After exchanging ideas back and forth, he mentioned that three of the other people working on the arrangement were Christians. All too aware of Eric's general disdain for anything "Christian," I quipped back, "How in the world did you ever find *them?*"

His response shocked me: "Well, what can I say? They're great people, and I love to be around great people."

Eric's words were a refreshing surprise to me. A hard-core agnostic befriending Christians because they are "great people" is a phenomenon that gives me pause in a day and age when these connections seem to be less frequent than ever. In light of the fact that Jesus befriended, interacted, ate, and conversed with "sinners," it seems clear by his own example that he wanted his followers to rub up against people who don't know him—not to preach and scold, but to listen and offer his truth and love. Jesus was holy, but he never separated himself from those he came to love.

I continue in relationship with Eric because I love him, regardless of his choices or beliefs. We no longer attempt to change each other. I am free to disagree with him and express my opinions, but I am more interested in loving him right where he is, hoping that someday he will discover the same need for Christ that I have. Dallas Willard eloquently sums up my sentiments: "To be the light of life, and to deliver God's life to women and men where they are and as they are, is the secret of the enduring relevance of Jesus."[2]

Perhaps this is where we have gone so far astray at times. I think we have too often tried to convince people of the relevance of the Christian religion rather than offering them Christ. There is a significant difference. Our faith should be an outflow of our relationship with Jesus, not the other way around. The former can too easily come across as a dry list of rules, dogma, or doctrine when presented apart from a personal love relationship with God himself.

The apostle Paul told the young church at Corinth something that I believe we too often forget in our determination to communicate the "truth":

> When I came to you, brothers, I did not come with
> eloquence or superior wisdom as I proclaimed to
> you the testimony about God. For I resolved to
> know nothing while I was with you except Jesus
> Christ and him crucified. I came to you in weakness
> and fear, and with much trembling. My message
> and my preaching were not with wise and persua-
> sive words, but with a demonstration of the Spirit's
> power, so that your faith might not rest on men's
> wisdom, but on God's power. (1 Corinthians 2:1-5)

Anyone who has read Paul's epistles is well aware that he had a lot to say about a lot of things. In chapter after chapter, he specifically addressed the early Christians regarding the way they should live—everything from learning how to love one another to how they should celebrate communion to what heaven would be like.

But those are issues he discussed with his fellow believers. Conversely, when he addressed those *outside* the church, he highlighted one thing alone: Jesus Christ and his sacrificial death to save the human beings he loved. Today I feel that we often reverse this. We tell people how they should live without first expressing and demonstrating to them the love and light of Jesus.

This issue has caused me a lot of distress as I have tried to reconcile my life within the Christian subculture with the realities of life on the outside. I wonder if my life has even a remnant of meaning and relevance to those who don't share my beliefs. I long for my life as a Christian to have an authentic flavor that causes people to hunger and thirst for the Source of my faith. I want to serve the best wine that has more to do with Jesus and less to do with what I've been taught that Christianity is "supposed" to look like. I want to offer others something deeper and richer and a little less predictable; something that will surprise even me; something I can't come up with simply by asserting my gifts and talents, or by trying harder; something that can only be explained as coming from the hand of God. Something much more like the wine the guests received at the wedding.

No Strings Attached

My friend Margaret has lived in the same house for more than fifteen years. She has a twelve-year-old neighbor who was born just a few years after Margaret moved into her home. Her name is

Caroline, and I've gotten to know her well. In fact, we had a barbeque at Margaret's just two nights ago, and Caroline was there. The morning before that she was over for toast. She stops by just about every day, feigning a few knocks as she slides through the foyer yelling, "Maaaarrgaret!" I wouldn't be surprised to find out that she has her own spare key.

Margaret's house is Caroline's second home, a place of respite and refuge where she can talk about the boys she has crushes on and about the friends she's going to miss over summer vacation while she teeters between being happy that she's out of school and being downright bored. She will readily tell you how thrilled she is to have Maggie as a friend, a role model, and someone she can look up to.

Last year I was over at Margaret's, touching up my makeup before going out to dinner with her. Caroline—to no one's surprise—was over and keeping me company as I reapplied my mascara. She began to tell me how fortunate I was. "You are sooooo lucky! You get to go to diiiiiiiiiinner with Margaret. Hang ooooooooout with Margaret. Go on vacaaaaaaaaation with Margaret. *And,* you get to be her good friend. BUT Margaret is even luckier than you…"

Clearly seeing where this was headed, I perked up. Obviously Caroline was about to tell me that Margaret was even luckier than I, because she gets to be *my* friend.

I couldn't have been more off.

Caroline's next words to me were—and I quote verbatim—

"Margaret is the luckiest one of all, because she gets to *beeeeeeee* Margaret."

Caroline has a point. Margaret does get to be herself, and for that she is very blessed, because we all think she's pretty great. Though my pride was momentarily bruised, I was happy that Caroline so highly esteems Margaret—not just because Margaret gets to be her amazing self, but because of the love she has consistently poured out on her young friend. Margaret has availed herself to Caroline in deep and costly ways. Margaret consistently demonstrates the love of Jesus as she sets aside her work, her social agenda, and her private time in order to establish and maintain a relationship with a young girl who is looking for what we all are looking for: someone who loves us unconditionally.

Margaret has given Caroline a Bible and has taken her to church, but not before spreading butter on her toast, or helping her press dried autumn leaves into a picture frame, or taking her to the park (not forgetting the mandatory stop at the food mart where Caroline likes to blend all the Slurpee flavors together for the perfect summer drink). I can't think of Margaret in this instance without thinking of Jesus, who boldly spoke of sin and repentance and righteousness and forgiveness, but not without touching the spotted skin of the leper, or raising a grieving mother's son to life, or filling the growling stomachs of thousands who had gathered on a hillside to hear his every word. He rarely delivered the message of the gospel without also responding to the tangible needs of the ones he was serving.

Margaret hopes that one day Caroline will understand the truest and most unconditional love of all: the love of Jesus that Margaret herself is merely a reflection of. I don't know where Caroline will ultimately land in her religious beliefs, but I do know for certain that Jesus and the Word of God will find a listening ear with Caroline because Caroline loves Margaret and trusts her. Margaret has offered Caroline her heart's desires, with no strings attached.

Similarly, Jesus not only served the wedding guests the best wine; he served them freely. He asked for no recognition, for nothing in return. And yet, somehow, the master of the banquet seemed to miss this. I often miss it in my own life, too, when I credit people for the wine that only Jesus can give.

7

WHERE CREDIT IS DUE

This chapter is giving me fits. I know this, because every five minutes I find myself abandoning my laptop for Thin Mints or to
change the temperature in the house by two degrees or to make
some phone call I've been putting off for weeks. Everything super-
fluous suddenly feels pressing, which is a telltale sign that I do not
want to write today. Perhaps more accurately, that I do not want
to write about this topic today.

I don't want to write about how we must find our "true wine"
in God alone. I don't want to write about how easy it is to depend
on other people or things or ideas, or whatever else, to provide this
wine. I don't want to write that what is on this "other" list never
truly satisfies the desires of our hearts. I am hesitant to wade in
these waters for at least two reasons to which I can boil down my
angst. First, I feel as if this subject has been addressed thousands of
times already—it's rhetoric that no longer gets a hearing. Second,

this is an area I have yet to get much of a handle on in my own life, so what can I, as a fellow struggler, offer others?

Sprinkled on top of these two obstacles are dashes of fear: I am afraid that if I write truth, my words will sound trite, but if I write from my heart, I will be in error. I want to write truth *and* what's in my heart, so I pray that somehow I will be able to strike a balance that will ring fresh upon your ears but fall sound upon your spirit. Right now—for the time being at least—I will say no to more Thin Mints.

I will ease into this topic by relaying a story. Last weekend I was in Florida over Valentine's Day, helping some new friends of mine with a florist shop they had just opened. I figure that if I'm not receiving flowers on Valentine's Day, I can console myself by delivering them. (Sadly, this wasn't very effective.) Anyhow, after a very long day of slicing my fingers, being pricked by thorns, and tying ribbons, I felt right at home. This was because my grandfather (whom I fondly refer to as "Pop") owned three florist shops while I was growing up. I am no stranger to such fascinating things as leaf-shining spray and green foam. I am a recordholder at such daring feats as how-long-can-you-stay-in-the-flower-cooler-before-you-freeze? But mainly, I am a flower-delivering whiz. I picked up this skill during successive summer vacations at my grandparents' house, when I regularly traded in a day at the beach for a day at the shops.

Looking back, I was peculiarly motivated by an entrepreneurial drive to make tip money that could (on good days) get me about a buck and a quarter. Pop would kindly send his delivery boys home early, taking me out on runs himself to indulge my delivery addiction. I have warm memories of the two of us careening through town (Pop is a very bad driver), pit-stopping at fabulous eateries like McDonald's. It was also our custom to hunt down Snickers bars by late afternoon—this being the climax of my day.

But sometimes Pop would forget about our Snickers breaks, and instead of asking him outright, I would subtly remind him by tossing out well-camouflaged questions like, "So, Pop, what's *your* favorite candy bar?"

On to my covert ways, he would stretch the game along by commenting back, "Ooooh, I don't know... I think I like Snickers best." He would leave it at that, interested to see what other tactics I might pull from my feeble arsenal.

Thinking, thinking, I would rhythmically stroke the corner of my lip with my pointer finger, eventually surfacing with another brilliantly disguised question like, "Do you get hungry for them when you're out on deliveries like we are?" And he would answer with another maddeningly dead-end response.

Back and forth we would go until he would notice that my suffering had reached an acute level and say the magic words, "You know, all this talk about Snickers bars is making me hungry. How 'bout we go get ourselves some?"

Often with chocolate in hand, I would whip open the cumbersome sliding door of the van, attempt to balance a floral arrangement that usually doubled the size of my body weight, then run my scrawny, somewhat athletic legs up to the doorstep—all in hopes that I would be generously remunerated. I'll just say it right now: People generally aren't good tippers when it comes to flowers. To this day, I'm not exactly sure what the protocol is, but if you see a pitiful, ten-year-old kid enthusiastically floundering up to your doorstep with flowers, throw him or her a dollar. The kid will never forget you.

Despite the fact that this gig didn't pay so well, I really enjoyed seeing people happy. I felt like a little elf, surprising people who were sick in the hospital, someone who had just turned forty, or people who weren't going through anything especially noteworthy but simply had a friend who wanted them to know they were loved. I got a kick out of people's reactions, though they were never really directed toward me. I was just the messenger. I was the means by which the best wishes of their friends and loved ones were delivered, but I wasn't the one who sent them. I brought the flowers, but they were not *from* me.

As an adult, I've had a hard time keeping these things straight; I get the deliverer confused with the sender. The same thing happened to the Israelites throughout the Old Testament, and it happened in the New Testament to the master of the banquet at Cana. The servants served him wine that originally was water, but Scripture adds a pivotal detail: "*He did not realize where it had come from,* though the servants who had drawn the water knew" (John 2:9, emphasis added).

I can't help but focus on the fact that the master—the guy in charge, the host of the gala—did not know where the wine had come from. The King James Version eloquently puts it this way: "[He] knew not whence it was." This is terribly sad to me—I picture the man delicately sipping the product of Jesus's first public demonstration of his miracle-working power, only to be sipping without knowledge. He cupped the container with his two hands, but he missed the person who filled it with the divine.

Ironically, the servants knew something the master did not. But perhaps what's even more interesting is that the master *thought* he knew. And this is where he made a common mistake—a mistake I take great comfort in knowing that someone who lived a little over two thousand years before me made. He credited man, not God: "*You,*" he said to the bridegroom, "have saved the best till now" (John 2:10, emphasis added). The master naively acknowledged the wrong "you." As if it were the bridegroom's wine! As if it had been his idea to save the best for last! The bridegroom had nothing to do with any of it, but the master filled in the blanks, crediting the bridegroom for such expensive wine, never considering that it might not have come from him—never discovering Jesus.

MISPLACED DEPENDENCIES

I see myself in the response of the master of the banquet. It is precisely what is so perplexing to me about my human nature. Despite the collective blessings and miracles the Lord has wrought in my life, I am continually tempted to drape his well-deserved accolades on a person or thing or circumstance. I find that it is far easier to credit a human for what God has done than to credit God for what God has done. And because he has so often expressed his love for me *through* other people, I have erred by looking exclusively to the individuals he has used, missing altogether that the blessing of his love all began with him. This is, tragically, so easy to do.

I was on a plane headed to Chicago the last time I stopped to ponder these truths. Whenever I travel by myself, especially for work, I tend to start feeling insecure about where I stand in my circle of friends. The first few days I'm generally fine, but, like clockwork, somewhere around the fourth day, my concerns start activating. I call home, moaning about how "out of the loop" I feel. I complain that I think things might be *chaaanging*. I wonder if everyone is truly able to function without me. (I am always surprised by how well they seem to manage.)

This trip was no different, though a favorite passage of mine in Hosea seemed to diffuse my fears for the time being. Thumbing through the first few chapters, I came across a curious quote. The Israelites said, "I will go after my lovers, who give me my food and my water, my wool and my linen, my oil and my drink" (2:5).

God responded, "She [Israel] has not acknowledged that *I* was the one who gave her the grain, the new wine and oil, who lavished on her the silver and gold…" (verse 8, emphasis added).

I was comforted by the simple reminder that it is *God* who lavishes me with modern-day versions of the aforementioned blessings. *He* is the One who has graciously built my friendships, and when I am traveling, he will continue to provide for me while safeguarding that which he has already so generously given. These verses took the panic out of my being away from home—where life feels safer and more dependable—while helping me put my concerns back into proper perspective. Ultimately, I was reminded anew of where my true wine originates. I mostly felt better until I landed—and then I forgot again.

So I find myself in good—but sort of bad—company with the master of the banquet and the Israelites. I am not alone in my proclivity to depend on others for the wine that only God gives. We have all heaped inappropriate praise or undue adoration upon a person for something God has done. And though the gesture may seem innocuous, it is an awful weight to sling around the neck of any human, because miracles can never come from them, or us. We pat people on the back for bringing out the finest wine at the eleventh hour when really they had nothing to do with it. It was simply their party, not their wine. We expect wine from them—or worse, we demand it—only to grow increasingly frustrated and disappointed when we realize they can't consistently provide what our hearts are starving for. We run back for more, holding out our empty cups, waiting for them to top us off. But they don't because they can't. They were never intended to be our source.

I have a friend who is literally caving under this kind of pressure right now. Friends and coworkers are clamoring for his time and attention, and he's simply unable to meet everyone's demands.

He is an incredibly strong and gifted person, but he is human, and he is wearing thin. Just the other day I heard him express his frustrations: "I am not God! I cannot be everyone's savior." The pressure that people were placing on him left him burdened by the only two conclusions he could draw: "I am a failure," and "I am someone who disappoints others." Neither is close to true.

I have seen a similar script being played out at times in the life of my dad, who has pastored a church for almost thirty years. Although a wonderful body of people surrounds him, he still has his fair share of overbearing and demanding folks who can unknowingly squeeze the life out of him. They assume that he has an endless supply of energy and is undaunted by their needs. They are surprised to find out that he does not own a red cape. Indeed, he is a great man, but he is just that, a man. He can only pour into people's cups what he has been given.

We have missed this point, I think, especially in our Christian communities, where we have put too high a premium on our leaders, athletes, singers, and so on. I see it all the time. Living in Nashville, where best-selling artists and singers are churned out by the dozens, grants me front-row seating for this type of thing. Part of the profits are based on convincing the public to believe that these are the people who need to be followed, acclaimed, and fervently sought after. We look to them to grant us what is impossible for them to generate on their own, subtly tempting them to believe that perhaps they do have such power. We place them on pedestals, leaving them with the choice the bridegroom had: to deflect the glory or pocket the accolades. It's a dangerous position for both sides.

THE TRUE WINE

As I reflect on my own life, I am all too aware of the many times I have fallen prey to such thinking. I see a slew of cups that I thought for certain would quench my thirst but instead left me dehydrating at their rim, primarily because I had mistaken the vessel for the Source. As I sit here this afternoon, I can call up the feelings of disillusionment and pain in a matter of moments, because the vessel has always ended up forsaking me, either cold-heartedly or simply out of an inability to meet my needs.

Right now a relationship of mine is shifting, changing, and I find that I am powerless to stop it. For many months it was right where I wanted it, but a new season has come. I am missing the give-and-take, the depth of this long-available friendship that was so rich but is absent, at least for the time being. All of life looks different to me now, and there is nothing I can do. I can keep demanding wine from a well that is dry—which only increases my angst and puts pressure on my friend—or I can echo the songs sung by one who found God sufficient in the midst of such times: "My soul finds rest in God *alone;* my salvation comes from him. He *alone* is my rock and my salvation; he is my fortress, I will never be shaken.… Find rest, O my soul, in God *alone;* my hope comes from *him*" (Psalm 62:1-2,5, emphasis added).

Sometimes it takes such drastic shifts and losses to get us looking back into the face of Jesus. Sometimes we have to endure the pain of change and uncertainty to rediscover that our well-being ultimately rests in God alone. I resist these moments like I resist my worst nightmares, but he loves me enough to bring them along anyhow. Some of my sweetest prayers are born at these crossroads, where I can embrace no one besides him. In my desperation, I have literally held my Bible to my chest, grasping at the sometimes agonizing truth that he is all I have. But how agony gives way to joy when I finally discover that he is more than enough!

I realize that as life continues to ebb and flow, I will cycle in and out of these times. Some seasons will resemble the one through which I am currently treading, when I experience more intimacy with God due to some losses and emptiness. But I know that I will once again enjoy a different kind of intimacy with him, an intimacy that stems from an abundance of external blessings and resources that will feel more present to me than they do right now. When those blessings come, I will have to take greater care in reminding myself that they are not coming from the "bridegroom," but from Jesus.

I type these words with vulnerable fingers because I have often been on the receiving end of some amazing blessings but have unwisely anchored my heart to them. It is a continual struggle to find the balance in all of these things. It is so much easier to rest my head on the shoulder of a friend than to fall into the invisible arms of God. *Of course it is.* Most days I'd rather hear the voice of my mom than strain at the silence on the other end of my prayers. But perhaps it is okay for these feelings to coexist in the same space. Perhaps they are not mutually exclusive. I struggle back and forth between depending on God as I know I should and my own natural tendency to run to other things. But I am slowly beginning to discover that maybe it's not so much about finding that perfect balance as it is about understanding where everything in my life comes from.

A small phrase in Hosea illustrates the blending together of God and his gift of relationships. He speaks in reference to the Israelites again, saying, "I led them with cords of *human* kindness" (11:4, emphasis added) or, as the King James Version says, "cords of a *man*." I see this as an expression that God understands our need to receive his love through human vessels. We naturally long for the feel of flesh and blood. We want tangible heroes and five fingers we can intertwine with our own. We love to see the face of Jesus in the face of our friends, our spouses, our parents. God gave us as gifts to one another, because he saw that it wasn't good for us to be alone (see Genesis 2:18).

God uses people. He grants us their companionship along the way. And with people in their rightful place, this is lovely and good—and just the way he intended it. But we must be careful to remember that every friend, every blessing, every gift, stems from the true Lover of our hearts. Everything we enjoy and rest upon for life falls into a sequential pattern that always leads back to God.

This morning I awoke to strong relationships, a healthy body, a career I love, and many other blessings upon which I can depend—for now. But I'm beginning to see more clearly that all of this is part of a greater whole that comes only from God. I will continue to call my mom and lean on my friends and enjoy the many blessings that are at my doorstep, but I hope I will continue learning to do so in the knowledge that, in and of themselves, they are not the Source. Rather, they are the jewels that fall from the Source's hands—the hands of Jesus.

I wonder if the master of the banquet ever made this connection. Did he ever discover that the true wine giver was Jesus? I wonder if the bridegroom ever confessed that it wasn't his wine or his idea to save the best for last. Scripture is strangely silent on these issues, but it leaves room for the imagination to do a little coloring. Mainly, it strengthens my resolve to not miss this connection in my own life.

In Christ Alone

I started this chapter almost a week ago, and I am still craving Thin Mints. I still want out of this topic, probably because it is one of my greatest weaknesses. My friends know this well. One in particular, whom I've known for a decade, consistently lets me know how I'm doing in this area. Tonia lives in London right now, which comes in handy if you want to do a little shopping overseas in the fashion capital of the world, but it isn't quite as convenient if you need someone to drop by and talk some sense into you. But her e-mails more than make up for the geographical distance between us.

Just moments ago I received a response to a note I had sent her describing my recent struggles with allowing the ebb and flow in my relationships and career path to dictate my sense of worth and adequacy. Add off-kilter hormones to the mix, and you'll have a good idea of what she was responding to.

Tonia began her rebuttal with "Kelly, Kelly, Kelly..." (My name written successively like this is never a good sign.) She patiently ran through the fundamentals with me yet again: My hope is in Christ alone; he has given me worth apart from everyone and everything else in which I tend to seek my definition; I have made far greater strides in this area than I am allowing myself to rest in.

It is good to be reminded of these things by people who know us—really know us. And since I can't fool them, I will honestly acknowledge the fact that I have not arrived at the top of the mountain. I cannot tell you from a bird's-eye view exactly how I got to where I am now, nor can I assure you unequivocally that if you just hang in there, the sunsets will be well worth your agony. I can't hand anyone a trail map to the summit, much less give away any shortcuts.

But slowly I am learning how to break the faulty pattern of searching for wine in something other than God, tapping that source dry, and then being devastated when I find that it cannot sustain me. I am learning more of what it means to find my wine in Christ *alone*. And when he lovingly allows others to deliver it for him, I'm discovering the joy of receiving from their hand without depending on them, or any number of bridegrooms, for my eternal supply.

Though, perhaps, one bridegroom would be nice.

8

STANDING FIRM

Today is the Fourth of July. Independence Day. As hot as the Sahara, but much more humid. I'm planning to run through my traditional routine, which means that in a few hours I'll be hovering around a grill—as if we're not hot enough already!—and eating really-bad-for-me foods that I will dip in even-worse-for-me sauces, which I will then do again and again. I'll stand around swatting at mosquitoes or my own tickling sweat that I have mistaken for mosquitoes. And I'll stay just long enough to seal the riveting experience by watching fireworks and the neighborhood kids lighting tanks and bottle rockets. Cracks and whistles and window-rattling booms will follow me into the night.

This year, however, I'm trying to change my perspective a bit. I mean, I'm still planning to swat my way through the whole heat-hamburger-sparkler shebang, but I want to make this event more personal—more meaningful to me.

I went running this morning and pondered how I might do this. As I jogged past patriotic paraphernalia and moms and dads out watering their gardens on what is normally a workday, I thought about the price of freedom. The many lives that have been given in exchange for me to have the opportunity to even go to barbeques. It's something we take for granted here in America. We just do. I'm not sure there's anyway we can't. We're as used to freedom as we are to the weather or running water or breathing. But it comes at a price nonetheless. An incredibly steep price that most of us don't begin to comprehend. So I decided I would spend the day not forgetting these things.

But as I considered the freedom I have as an American citizen, I couldn't stop there. I began to follow that train of thought to my own heart. *How free am I here?* I mused. I thought of those areas in which I feel bound, those heavy cords that I can't seem to unloose. I began wondering if, over the years, I had become any freer, mainly because it seems that I'm always battling the same demons: fear, selfishness, jealousy, insecurity, etc. I concluded that, yes, I have been freed of much, but I also recognize that some things will never stop constricting me at some level. I am a *human* being, after all.

Running…thinking…walking…running, running, running again to get away from the bite-size poodle that snaps at my heels *every* time I pass by the house she guards. When she finally turned back, I returned to my thoughts… *I wish that on this Fourth of July*

I could have a private celebration of my own soul-freedom. I committed to viewing the day as a personal holiday for me as a struggling, but liberated person. I haven't wiggled out of every cage or broken free from every fetter, but I am grateful for the progress that has been made and in awe of the price that has been paid.

FIGHTING FOR FREEDOM

Paul wrote to the Christians in Galatia, "It is for freedom that Christ has set us free. Stand firm, then, and do not let yourselves be burdened again by a yoke of slavery" (Galatians 5:1). This enlightens me in a way I wouldn't have expected: We have to *stand firm* in our freedom. Liberty isn't something that just happens or is sustained without our continual attention. I think of our own country and the liberty we have achieved. Since we established our independence, we have never for one moment had the luxury of sitting back and just allowing things to take their course. We have protected ourselves, because freedom is not something that "just is." It is not a one-time achievement on which we can casually rely. We have to tend to it and fight for it because bondage and slavery will never cease to be a threat. Our freedom must be worked for.

I imagine that Independence Day means more to my grandfather than to most people. A retired Navy admiral, he risked his life for days like today. He lost friends and left loved ones for months at a time to secure our nation's liberty. When he watches the annual fireworks, I'm sure he sees more than flashing colors that decorate the night sky. I'm sure he stands at attention, remembering long nights at sea, close calls as a pilot, and faces of those who are no more. He knows firsthand that the cost of liberty is the laying down of lives. In order for us to live, some must die.

It is really no different in the spiritual realm. In order to save our lives, we must lose them. Whoever loses his life will find it. A seed must go into the ground and die before it can spring to new life. These are the eloquent, yet painfully difficult-to-hear truths that Jesus spoke into existence. Though I wish there were another way, the lose-your-life-so-you-can-find-it path is the only way I've found to freedom.

No matter how we dress up the Christian faith or how appealing we try to make Christianity sound, and no matter how many charming books are written or slick television sermons are preached, at the core of it all is this one huge, irrevocable principle: For us to be free, we must submit ourselves to God. We cannot do this while we are still trying to be our own masters. Soul-freedom requires obedience and servanthood and, ultimately, surrender, and every other requirement that drives me crazy, until I remember that these "religious" responses are not life squelching, but are routes to liberation.

But the path to freedom can be arduous. In fact, writing this chapter has taken me to task. I found myself in a really bad mood yesterday the minute I sat down to write on this subject, and it didn't lift until I shut down my laptop for the night. I came toe to toe with the fact that soul-freedom is not easy to achieve and that bondage tends to be my default mode. We all have things we allow to hold us captive for a litany of reasons. And it never fails...just when I think I'm getting a handle on these things, I lose my grip altogether.

For example, I just found out that I'm about to head out on a radio promotional tour that will take the greater part of the next two months to finish. Immediately after that, I leave for a twenty-city tour that will be interspersed with an additional ten or so solo dates. All of this will take me right up to Thanksgiving, and today is only the Fourth of July! Within an instant, my summer and fall seem to have disappeared.

I'm keeping a cool, confident front with my manager and record company, but deep down this terrifies me. I don't want to leave home. I'm not looking forward to being away from the close-knit community I have developed here in town. I don't want to miss out on walks in the park or going out for Italian with my friends. And I don't want to skip an entire season of Sunday-afternoon football or get back after the leaves have already changed and fallen. My friends have become my extended family, and it's unsettling for me to leave them again. The great big mother-fear is that I will be lonely. It is the overarching fear under which every other fear of mine falls.

Thinking about these things prompted me to leaf through my

journals and read about the last thirty-five-city tour I took in the fall of 2001. Every night I would record my thoughts lying down, since the bunks on the bus were too shallow for anyone to sit up in (think coffin). The name of a different city headed each entry: White Oak, Texas; Lexington, Kentucky; Hastings, Nebraska; and on my birthday, some city in South Dakota that I forgot to note, probably because I was so sad about spending it there that I blanked it out altogether.

The prospect of traveling again feels so depressing to me. In fact, I feel a bit panicked. I'm not sure I want to go out and pound the pavement again, and then again, and then some more. I'm not looking forward to afternoons spent in bad hotels, or delayed flights when I'm desperate to get home, or cell phone calls that break up one-sentence exchanges into a thousand digital pieces. I want familiar faces and conversations with no interruptions—not, "Can you hear me now?" I want the comfort of my community. I want my own bed.

Perhaps my reactions are a little exaggerated, or perhaps this would be stressful for anyone. I've been living this vagabond, entrepreneurial lifestyle for too long to have an objective perspective on how "normal" my feelings are. But either way, they are still rooted in fear, and when it comes to fearing loneliness, I find it to be my Achilles heel. It has dogged me since childhood.

As a kid I was afraid to go to school. Afraid for my mom to leave me. Afraid she wouldn't pick me up. Afraid that I wouldn't know what to do or that I would have no one to sit with. I tried hard to cover up these fears, but I quickly discovered that I was not Broadway bound for my acting abilities. My hands trembled in kindergarten; tears from being left would uncontrollably slip out until I could pull myself together and tuck them in again. And that was *before* having to ride the bus to elementary school. Getting on *that* thing for the first time felt like a death wish. What kind of guarantee did I have that this perfect stranger would actually take me to school and back home again? For all I knew, she might drive me to the hills of West Virginia and push me out onto the side of the road, separating me from my family forever. I thought long and hard about these threatening possibilities.

Of course, as I've matured and grown in confidence over the years, I'm a little less phobic. But the fears haven't gone away. I wear them with a little more class, and they're slightly more masked, but if it were fully acceptable—and I knew in advance that no one would judge me—I would cry out in the most obnoxious, whimpering, childish voice, "Don't make me go! Don't make me go! Pleeeeeeease don't make me go!"

I haven't resorted to this yet, but it's everything I'm thinking and feeling. I hold back the "I'm-falling-apart" drama, not so much because I'm afraid of what people might think, but because I know I *have* to go. Not just because I have to make a living and this is the only way I know how to do it, and not just because I have to hold up my end of the bargain with my record company and booking agency; but because I know that this is what God has put in my heart to do. I'm confident of this, and even though I'm afraid at times, I can't curl up like a pill bug because I don't want to leave home.

But choosing the high road doesn't keep all my anxiety at bay. It just means that I lay down my own agenda and fears for the sake of doing what I believe God is asking of me. I have stretched in these areas a great deal, but I'm not sure that it will ever be easy for me to step on a bus or board a plane at the expense of being away from so much I hold dear. But this is where the fight for freedom comes in. In obedience and trust there is liberty. It doesn't mean that everything is suddenly better for me, but that my fears don't dictate my decisions. It's not that I don't fear, it's just that my fears aren't the controlling factor.

Freedom in Christ is similar, at least in my experience. Again, I think we as a Christian community do ourselves (and others) a great disservice when we promote the idea that freedom from our struggles is an instantaneous event, a one-time moment of deliverance. Paul's statement in Galatians 5:1—"It is for freedom that Christ has set us free"—refers to the instantaneous part: Jesus Christ hung on a cross to bear the sins of the world in order to secure our eternal freedom. But the second part of Paul's statement cautions us that day-to-day freedom in our mortal bodies is something we must vigorously protect. We must hold our ground so we do not slip back under the heavy burdens that hold us captive.

Maintaining our soul-freedom is up to us. Based on my own

experience as well as the experiences of those who are farther down the road than I am, it's a lifelong battle. It is supposed to be hard. Acknowledging that challenge relieves me because it is far more stressful to think that being a Christian guarantees automatic victory or immediate deliverance from something that we will never have to work at again—especially considering the fact that I have never been able to accomplish this struggle-free way of life. Yet this incorrect way of thinking continues to be propagated and has led to the destruction of many Christians who are sincere followers of Christ but have had to work desperately hard for their freedom.

Walking freely is not about walking without struggle; it is about walking without our struggles controlling us. As we are transformed into the image of Christ and continue to be obedient, I think that certain things become—dare I say—easier. Our gnawing fears and addictions and our wayward tendencies aren't so overpowering. I think we develop a greater capacity to trust God each time we step out in faith and overcome our urges to act otherwise. We may walk with a limp, but we walk nonetheless.

Does this not reflect the story of the thorn in Paul's side that God refused to take away? Or of Mephibosheth, who was lame but sat at the king's table? Or of Moses, who stuttered but did not allow his impediment to keep him from obeying God and confronting Pharaoh? These people were not free of weighty problems, but they did not succumb to them in the end. That is the victory I am seeking in my own life.

Eagles' Wings

I had just arrived at a remote camp in New Jersey where I was going to perform that night. I discovered that my cell phone had no signal, so I realized I was probably farther away from civilization than I wanted to admit. My first tip-off was when—on the way from the airport—we passed a packed-out rodeo in a place called "Cowtown." I was hoping this alarming sight was not a precursor of things to come.

After arriving, I found my thoughts drifting back to family vacations when I was a kid. Set on a lake, the camp reminded me of all I loved about our summer getaways together. I suddenly felt no loyalties to my guitar or luggage and abandoned them to a stranger so I could go for an exploratory walk. First stop: a tantalizing row of kayaks. More like an eager kid, and less like the hired entertainment for the evening, I asked the promoter if I could take one out for a spin before sound check. He handed me a paddle.

I had never kayaked before, so the oar became a potentially dangerous tool in my hands. I remained undeterred, however, and coasted out onto the open water, allowing the fresh breeze to rejuvenate me after breathing the regurgitated air on the plane. I propped my legs up on the outside of my new vessel and smugly thought (at least on calm waters), *I am a natural.*

I cut through the water like a nautical veteran. I also sailed past several buoys that signified a no-trespassing zone. For some reason I missed that whole subliminal message, and without a care in the world, I curved around the bend, reassuring myself that being on the road is not so bad after all—even when you're playing venues where there is no cellular service and the next city over is Cowtown.

Blissfully ignorant and floating into forbidden waters, I was suddenly mesmerized by something I hadn't seen in years: a bald eagle. Gliding through the air, the eagle made my sleek kayak maneuverings seem stunted. Motionless, I watched her fly to a nearby tree and perch there for several seconds. Either finding what she was looking for or getting bored, the eagle then flew off into the invisible distance. This sight was the cherry on top of an already spectacular view.

After soaking in the experience, I decided to race back to shore before it was too late to rehearse. I had barely slipped out of the kayak when a woman came running up to me, asking if I had seen the eagle. (With one question, she single-handedly deflated my excitement; I thought *I* had been the first to see it.) Turns out, the string of buoys on the lake was specifically intended to deter people from disturbing the eagle's nest. Apparently the eagle I saw was, with her mate, one of only thirty-five pairs of eagles in New Jersey, all of them on the endangered list.

As I walked back to my "dressing room" (okay, it was a lodge), I couldn't help but view my experience against the backdrop of all I've been writing about. The eagle—the very symbol of freedom—

needed to have her freedom protected. Protected from overzealous kayakers who pay no heed to buoys. An entire infrastructure had been put into place to safeguard the eagle, keep her and her mate reproducing, and enable her to fly without limits.

I can only imagine what would become of the eagles without that special protection. I am very aware of what happens to me when I let down my own defenses, when I decide that protecting my freedom in Christ is simply not worth the effort. I quickly sink into a spiritual lethargy, and all my "natural" responses take over. I forget that I am in desperate need of Christ, and I become self-reliant and self-absorbed. I take offense at things more easily and tend to miss the bigger picture of what God is up to in my life and in the world.

Mostly, I am rendered useless for anything of eternal value. Life begins to be all about *me,* which is a heavy weight to bear. When I am consumed with my own desires and agendas and am seeking wholeheartedly to fulfill them, then it's entirely up to me to satisfy their demands. I have no other choice; I am responsible for them. This means I end up answering to no one but myself, manipulating others to give me what I need, and overriding what God might have me do simply because I have these "other things" that I am now responsible for. It is a burdensome cycle that is anything but free.

Again, Paul reminds me not to slip back underneath this heavy burden—the yoke of slavery. But this requires a firm stance, a plan of action, and effort on my part. Sometimes I tire of it, but I have to remind myself that I will always be a slave to something, whether to Jesus or to someone or something else. Only slavery to Christ yields freedom; everything else brings bondage.

The servants at the wedding in Cana demonstrate this truth. First, they were obedient when it didn't make sense (filling water pots when they needed jugs of wine). Had they been operating out of their finite understanding, they would never have carried water to the wedding master, knowing he was expecting wine. Second, their obedience was complete—they filled the jugs "to the brim." They carried out their task responsibly and with honor; they did nothing halfway. And, in the end, their reward was full, as they shared in the glorious secret of the wine. But isn't it interesting that the glory of the servants' being part of a miracle and the intimacy of their being in on a secret didn't come by any other means than their being servants of Jesus. Technically, the servers looked like slaves, but in reality they were free. Free to know secrets, free to be part of the mysterious, free to follow, free of themselves. They represent the ultimate dichotomy: They were *free servants*. Which is what I believe we are all called to be.

This freedom requires that we make a concerted effort to protect our "eagle's nest," though our individual methods will probably look unique to each of us. For me, protection is comprised of many elements: a community I can be honest with, a pastoral couple who looks after me, the prayer and support of family and friends, honest and regular dialogue with Jesus, a surrendering posture before him, along with less overtly "spiritual" things such as exercise and walks in the park, laughter, spending time with children and pets, music, play…and I would like to justify including good pasta somewhere on the list.

I am committed to these things because I am committed to my freedom. I need all of these hedges of protection so that I will not be overly hampered by my *self,* because there is no doubt that *I* am my biggest obstacle to freedom. Each one of these protections encourages me to remain focused on Christ. For me, this doesn't mean spending all day every day reading Scripture and meditating. It means that when I get inordinately worried about finances, I call my pastor and let him know I'm discouraged. It means that when I'm overtaken by self-pity, I grab dinner with a friend who will remind me of the wonderful ways God has shown himself faithful to me thus far. It means that when I'm at my wit's end with my own weaknesses and struggles, I quietly (or loudly) pray, pleading for supernatural change. And it also means that when I'm burned out and tired, I go for a run and then gorge myself on rigatoni with pesto and sun-dried tomato cream sauce with pine nuts—which always makes me feel better.

My "liberty list" is ultimately about surrender. It is about holding out my open hands to the Lord, ready to move or stay or lay something down or pick up something new as he leads. It is about being docile in his hands with a childlike trust that, wherever God is leading me, it will ultimately be good. Because it is for freedom that Christ has set me free. Because I want to run and not be weary, to walk and not faint. Mostly, it is because I want to fly with wings like eagles.

For this, I will stand firm.

9

MEMORY SERVES

I have a personal milestone coming up: my ten-year anniversary of keeping a journal. It's filled with everything from embarrassing moments to touching scriptures to tear-stained accounts of heartbreak to revelations and error and truth and anger and joy. It contains smatterings of life. My life. Bits and pieces of my journey recorded over the course of a decade.

When people find out that I'm a journaler, they often ask me what kind of journals I write in and how many I have. I have never really considered such things, as I have not been frilly about the process. I have stuck to college-ruled paper that I place in a blue three-ring binder. At the end of each year, I proudly pull out January through December, tap the pages on a hard surface to align the edges, then slip them into a manila folder and file them successively according to year.

Suddenly I am realizing how drab this sounds. Maybe during

the next ten years I will try my hand at floral hardbacks or, even better, leather-bound journals. More than likely, however, I will return to my trusty blue binder. It's entirely too functional to abandon. I guess that's why I began journaling in the first place: It serves a specific function…to help me remember. I was afraid of forgetting something in particular.

It was during my freshman year of college, amidst all the awkwardness and instability—basically junior high personified—when I really began to struggle with "life." I can't be any more specific than that because it wasn't only one thing I was struggling with. It was all the little things that prompt you to put on extra makeup in the morning, or pay more attention to your outfits, or go to more Bible studies, or try to win more friends—anything to abate the rumblings inside.

Up to that point I had been living with a profound void regarding God's love for me. I had experienced some hurtful and monumentally negative moments in my life that left me with an invisible wall around my heart that I couldn't seem to let God penetrate. I viewed him as austere and saw the Christian life as little more than ascetic living that allowed scant earthly pleasure or joy. Despite my best attempts, I felt that I could never measure up to my Creator's expectations.

As I was reading through Scripture one morning, I came across a verse that initiated a profound change in me. It caused me not only to know but to *feel* the love of God for the first time in my life. The verse was seemingly obscure, tucked away in the often lengthy passages of Deuteronomy: "The LORD your God…turned the curse into a blessing for you, because the LORD your God loves you" (23:5).

I can't really describe the moment except to say that it was one of those times when Scripture leaped off the page and brought me to tears. I was intimately touched by a promise that God seemed to be making to me personally. I was suddenly and profoundly convinced of his care. His love dripped down into the cavernous places of my heart, letting me know that he was intimately aware of everything I had considered to be a curse and that he would not stop at simply removing it, but was actually going to transform it into a blessing. Why? Because he LOVES me. This was astounding news. Head-news that I had known for years but was only now discovering as heart-news. There was simply no denying the reality of the encounter, and no mistaking God's voice.

As I closed my Bible, I felt compelled to seal the experience—to drive a stake into the ground and ensure that my promise from God would not be stolen by the thief of forgetfulness. That's when I began putting pen to paper, experience to story, promise to ink—so I would remember. Because remembering, much like freedom, is not something that just happens. David's desperate prayer in Psalm 143 makes it clear that remembering God's faithfulness is not only critical to our spiritual journey, but it's something we have to work at—especially when we feel "faint" or "dismayed," as the psalmist did (verse 4). Overwhelmed by these feelings, David made a choice: "I remember the days of long ago; I meditate on all your works and consider what your hands have done. I spread out my hands to you; my soul thirsts for you like a parched land" (verses 5-6).

SPIRITUAL AMNESIA

Several weeks ago I bought a gift for my friend Debi that I keep forgetting to give her. Knowing I was going to see her last night, I set the package right next to my front door in the early afternoon so that I'd be sure not to leave it behind again. In spite of my own brilliant tactics, I not only walked right by it, but I actually nudged it out of the way so I could get out the door more easily. Needless to say, my friend is still without her new shoes, and I am still memory-challenged.

My poor memory is even worse in the spiritual realm. I have not one stone to throw at the Israelites for their collective forgetfulness as they wandered in the desert. I can say nothing against the disciples who doubted Jesus and scattered when he was arrested, even though they had watched him turn water into wine. You see, it turns out that there were at least a handful of others besides the servants at the wedding in Cana who also knew where the wine had come from: "[Jesus] manifested...his glory; and *his disciples* believed on him" (John 2:11, KJV, emphasis added).

Clearly Jesus's closest followers had believed in him prior to witnessing his miracle at the wedding. But seeing his wonder-working power in action caused them to believe in a whole new way. Their faith became more personal and settled. According to the King James Version, there is a difference between believing *in* Jesus and believing *on* him. I am learning the difference in my own life. I'm afraid I live most days believing *in* him, yet how can I forget the moments where the mundane has turned to the divine, where dreams have turned to reality, where the miraculous has grazed the surface of earth, and I have found myself believing *on* him? These things have happened, and my faith has been strengthened, and I have remembered…until the sneaky crook of hardship pulls me back into fear, and then my hope wanes, and my belief fades, and I stop believing on him and just believe in him, and…I forget. And I despair. And I become like David and the Israelites and the disciples.

Peter was quick to deny, Thomas was given to doubt, Judas betrayed with a kiss, and the whole lot of them feared the storm on the Sea of Galilee even though Jesus was aboard their small craft. The disciples jostled for position, wondering who would be first in Jesus's kingdom. They were at a complete loss as to how the multitude's hunger would be satisfied. All this uncertainty in spite of seeing with their own eyes the wine that a moment before had been water.

I would like to think that if I'd had the luxury of walking with Jesus in the flesh and witnessing the supernatural in the midst of the natural, I would never have doubted or questioned or betrayed or denied. Yet I'm convinced that my heart is just as dull as the hearts of the disciples. Because I have seen the hand of God in my life—instances that are almost as tangible as water becoming wine—and yet I have been just as quick to forget as those before me, behaving as if I had seen nothing at all.

My music career has been full of such occasions. When I was first starting out, I had no money and no resources. I banged out songs on a hundred-dollar classical guitar that my mom and dad had shared in college. It was no wonder that my eye had wandered to a brand new Gibson on display at the local music shop. The wafer-thin price tag was the only thing standing between us.

It was Christmastime, and someone in our church had anonymously left a check on my dad's desk; it "happened" to be for the exact price of the guitar. Secretly, Dad drove to the music store and walked away with my dream Christmas gift in hand. He laid it in an open case on the stairs leading up to our living room. It was the first thing I saw upon entering the house, and the last thing everyone heard me playing that night.

Years later I was in need of a second guitar—something even more refined and expensive. I was barely scraping by and didn't have the extra money to invest, so even though I window-shopped every chance I got, I pretty much had to shelve the desire. That is until an unassuming couple approached me after a concert one night and asked me if there was anything I needed. I politely told them that I was perfectly taken care of and that, no, there was nothing.

They persisted. "Anything? Anything at all? We have money, and we'd like to contribute to what you're doing."

I didn't know what to say. I felt mildly uncomfortable, as I had never laid eyes on them before. But after I kept assuring them that I was taken care of and they kept insisting that there must be *something* I could use, I finally succumbed. "Well, if you *really* want to know…I mean, this is absurd really, but (hem-haw)…I'm looking for a new guitar."

They didn't flinch, but I kept stumbling forward: "I'm sure that's not what you meant when you said you wanted to help. I'm sure that's about fifteen hundred dollars more than what you were thinking. It's silly, really, but since you asked…" And within a few days, I was holding the most amazing guitar I had ever laid eyes on. I haven't seen the couple since.

I have pages and pages of this kind of stuff. God has continued to send these assurances along the way, though half the time you wouldn't know it by listening to me. I have gotten excessively downcast at times. I have felt forsaken by God at many junctures in the road. I have found myself wondering if he brought me to Nashville only to send me back to Virginia. Or if he brought me here just to squelch my spirit. I have remembered through the distorted lenses of the Israelites: "Oh, how much better things were where I came from! Did you bring me out of D.C. just so I could starve here in the South?"

I know I am prone to forgetfulness. I have a short-term memory, or sometimes just an inaccurate one. I have experienced the intimate touch of God one moment, only to stray or demand or fear the next. I am prone to look forward, sometimes desperately, for my provision, forgetting how much peace and blessing come from looking backward and recalling his faithful loving-kindness.

GREAT IS THY FAITHFULNESS

Maybe part of my tendency to forget stems from the American culture I live in and the way we are taught to focus on the immediate. We spend our energies on the here and now even as we vigorously plan for the future. Minimal regard is given to the past. We live for instant gratification, and we dream about what's ahead. But we spend little time thinking about and being amazed and encouraged by what is behind.

My friends and I have a favorite birthday tradition: We sit around a fabulous meal and talk about our best memories of the particular friend we are celebrating. We tell stories, both funny and serious. We share our most memorable experiences from years past, everything from the simple and silly to the experiences that have had the deepest impact on us. This time of remembrance is always the highlight of the evening. It reminds each of us of our place in life, the bigger picture, and God's story as a whole. I can look forward to turning twenty-nine years old because of what I learned while I was twenty-eight.

Our future seems to lose its meaning without the grounding of our past. One of the many reasons I love being with my grand-parents is because I love to hear about days gone by, and how things "used to be," and what their parents were like, and who they dated, and where they traveled, and anything else I can get out of them with a bit of cajoling. I recently sat with my grandfather over seafood on the shores of Annapolis. It's the perfect combination: artichoke-crab dip and Navy stories from Admiral Grandpa. What could be better?

During a recent conversation, he relayed an exceptional story of a fellow admiral friend named Chuck, who spent several years in solitary confinement as a prisoner of war in Vietnam. He was missing long enough for his family to assume he was dead and move on without him. When Chuck finally returned to the United States, he brought with him a seemingly photographic memory that has baffled my grandfather for years. Every time the two of them reminisce about old friends and servicemen, war stories, and detailed incidents from their young-adult lives, my grandfather has difficulty remembering much of what Chuck brings up in conversation.

Recently, after stretching his memory to its limit, my grandfather finally asked, "Chuck, how *do* you remember these things?"

Chuck's response was simple. "Charlie, if you had spent seven years in the confines of a cell in complete solitude, you would remember too."

His answer gave me chills. Chuck's memory was the only thing that connected him to his life back home. Remembering gave him a sense of self and a frame of reference. If he ever forgot, he would be left with nothing.

Similarly, I cannot afford to forget my spiritual journey with the Lord. If I did, I would lose my perspective, my frame of reference, and eventually my way. Because remembering the past provision of God increases my faith for the present and the future. Every time I face my own demons or fears, I can recall God's past deliverances. I remember a particular season when he was silent for an unbearable stretch of time, and I thought he had left me. But then he spoke and I was comforted. I remember when he said no to a fervent request but later said yes to something I didn't even know I wanted, but now I can't imagine living without. All of these trials and deliverances serve to bolster my faith and trust.

My journal writing serves as a joist that upholds my memory. It is my Ebenezer or *stone of help,* as Samuel so aptly named the rock that signified the place where God had saved him and given his troops victory (1 Samuel 7:12). As often as I can, I lay down my own Ebenezers on paper; they serve as memorials for me, helping me to remember what God has done in my life. We can find comfort in the present by remembering our past.

I've become convinced that it is imperative to find ways to remember because remembering our past determines how we will experience the future. I have chosen to remember good times in the midst of hard times, and hard times in the midst of good times, because I gain perspective from both. When I was muddling through the long stretch without a record deal, and everyone seemed to be closing their doors on me, and I wasn't sure how I would pay my bills, I read back through my journal and remembered God's faithfulness to me during similar difficulties in the past. I found encouragement that strengthened my resolve to keep pressing forward.

As things have begun to look up for me and there is more opportunity on the table and a record deal in the bag, I have chosen to read back over the valleys and dips I recorded in my journal. These experiences remind me of what a blessing it is to be here and how God's hand has brought me here, not my own. It helps me to not take anything for granted.

Deuteronomy is one of my favorite books in the Bible, especially because of its emphasis on remembrance. Chapter 8 is full of God's admonitions to the Israelites to remember all that he had done for them before they entered the Promised Land. He knew that once the honey started flowing and the milk began running, his chosen people would be likely to forget their desert wanderings and his provision along the way. He knew they would be inclined to think that their newly acquired power and wealth were the results of their own efforts rather than gifts from him.

When God tenderly reminded them of all he had done, he mentioned something that deeply touches me. He told them not to forget the manna he had fed them in the wilderness—the manna that their forefathers had never tasted (see Deuteronomy 8:16). This nourishment was a specific provision for the Israelites while they wandered in the desert. Abraham, Isaac, and Jacob had never tasted the "bread of angels" that sustained their descendants for decades. They had never peered out of their tents at a landscape miraculously covered with fresh food. This event, never seen before or since, was unique to the desert-wanderers. God had graced the Israelites in ways that even their stalwart forefathers had not experienced, and he didn't want them to forget these unique blessings.

Manna from Heaven

My most meaningful times with the Lord have come as a result of his gift of "manna" to me—personal provisions that others know little or nothing about. We all have secret longings and desires that are so personal to us that we barely know how to speak them. So when God meets us in these places that are beyond description and beyond what even our spouses or closest friends understand about us, we are touched by the intimacy of a Friend who "sticks closer than a brother" (Proverbs 18:24). It has been my joy, and my discipline, to record such moments so I will never be robbed of their treasures.

Just yesterday I awoke in the quiet hours of the morning, somewhat harried by my teeth grinding and the ruckus of some scurrying animal in the attic whose alarm had clearly gone off before mine. The day before had been rough, and the subconscious lull of a night's sleep hadn't distanced me enough from it. I concluded that I had been overly focused on myself—or maybe too aware of myself is a more accurate description. Too caught up in how I was doing as a person, as a Christian, as a friend. I envisioned a seam running down the middle of my life: On one side I could see where I was succeeding; on the other side, where I was failing.

As I pondered this state of affairs, I felt the Holy Spirit gently tugging at my heart, nudging me to lay down my perceived successes and failures and simply lift my gaze to him. This was my desire, but I couldn't seem to do it. I was in need of manna. Hearing from God was imperative. Remembering who he is and believing *on* him as the disciples did in Cana became essential for me.

So I prayed and opened my Bible to Matthew 17, peering in on a few of the disciples as they witnessed Christ's transfiguration. Peter was there on the summit of a secluded mountain, along with James and John and two celestial visitors, Moses and Elijah. Peter, in his usual, awkward way, was suggesting that he could build tabernacles for Moses, Elijah, and Jesus. In fact, as Jesus was being transformed before them, and as Moses and Elijah were reappearing from beyond the grave, Scripture says, "Then *answered* Peter…" (verse 4, KJV, emphasis added). Interestingly enough, no one had been asking any questions!

I greatly appreciate the humanness of Peter and his insatiable need to execute a plan or have a suitable answer, even if no one is asking. What amuses me more is that when God began to speak out of heaven and a bright cloud "overshadowed" the men, Scripture says that it happened *while Peter was still speaking!* In the midst of glory and holiness and mystery and, oh yes, Peter's infamous speaking, the disciples fell on their faces in sheer terror and humility when God spoke. And here is what blesses me more than anything: "And when they had lifted up their eyes, they saw no man, *save Jesus only*" (verse 8, KJV, emphasis added).

"Save Jesus only." Those words became my manna. It was the very thing God had been whispering to me: "Look at me, Kelly, and you will see nothing else." Before the disciples heard God's voice loud and clear, they were full of plans and wonder and fear; but when God cracked the outer glass of their world, they saw only Christ. No one else.

That is all I needed yesterday—to be reminded that God is capable at any time of manifesting how much "more" he is than any concern in my life. Especially, how much more he is than me. My prayer as I left my bed yesterday morning was, "May you descend upon my life so that all of my cares and questions and burdens will be enveloped by your magnificence, that I might see nothing but you."

I am writing this down so I won't forget it. I want to remember the ways God has spoken to me, and I simply don't always realize the extent of what he has so graciously done and how he has so specifically moved in my life until I start writing…until I start remembering. Maybe this is why journaling is one of the few disciplines I've been able to maintain for so long. Experience after experience, blessing after blessing, joy after joy, grief after grief— they are the amalgamation of the story God is writing with my life. It's a story I don't want to forget, because with every closing of my journal, I experience a renewed confidence and peace. My worries about the present never seem as pressing when I receive the comfort that comes from remembering the past. This makes me want to read through my journals more often. It makes me want to write so I can read more, so I can remember more—so I don't forget. I don't want to heedlessly slip into the mind-set of the disciples who saw water become wine but then saw only obstacles: a storm that tossed their boat, famished people with only a few loaves and fishes, a hopelessly ailing woman, a cross that held their King. How quickly they forgot the mystery that lay beneath it all: Jesus only.

Oh that I might not forget water becoming wine, new guitars for Christmas, manna from God, verses from Scripture…and to write in my blue binder.

10

GLASS CLINKING VERSUS
WATER DRAWING

When I decided to move to Nashville, I left the white-collar, yuppie computer world for the avant-garde, bohemian art community. I went from a group of people who worked well within the nine-to-five, Monday-through-Friday framework to a bevy of free-thinkers who began their workdays whenever they woke up, often plowing through the night—Saturdays, Sundays, and Christmas—whenever inspiration hit.

Though I wouldn't categorize myself as supremely artsy or even all that forward thinking, I function far better within the latter system. I feel right at home here and find that Nashville has influenced me more than I would like to admit: I'm drinking soymilk, visiting art galleries, burning candles at breakfast… I'm less business-casual and more unconventional-eccentric. I've left PCs for Apples, politics for country music. But in my early days here I embraced at least one change that did not prove as benign as computers or clothing. Definitely not as healthy as soymilk. Something I should not have gotten used to. Something that has caused me angst as I have forged my way through the infamous music business. I call it "glass clinking."

This is my own little made-up term. It's how I describe the superficial nature of an industry that is based primarily upon image, status, perception, glamour, and so on. It can be a who's-who, flavor-of-the-month club that leaves most everyone out, save an elect few who happen to be "aligning with the taste of the times," as a friend describes it.

Glass clinking. It's what I came to Nashville to do. Well, not exclusively. It was well masked with nobler goals, such as wanting to impact people, bring glory to God, and write music that brings healing and conviction, among other things. These were legitimate and authentic desires that still fuel my passion to create art today. And yet, hiding underneath it all was the truth that I *wanted* to glass clink. I wanted to be known and sought after. I wanted to dine backstage at awards shows, show up on VIP lists, have chart-topping singles and favorable press. I wanted to *be* Somebody. And if it was possible to hold a glass and clink it—whatever picture of success that brought to my mind—I was willing to stop at little to get there.

I coined my little term while pondering the servants' humbling task of drawing and delivering water in a room full of party-ing guests. Because servants do not represent the things we are after as ladder-climbing individuals, we tend to view them as those who hover somewhere beneath the bottom rung—and we pray that God will not assign us their position. But how skewed is our thinking! God's view of servanthood is completely the opposite of our own.

Moving to a town that has built an entire industry on glass clinking has caused me to think through what I'm living for and what is ultimately important. This task has been anything but easy. In fact, it has resulted in an all-out dismantling and rebuilding of everything I came here intending to do. Overhauling my perspec-tive and desires is not something I could have accomplished on my own—not to mention that I didn't see a need to. Why alter my desires when I was certain they would bring me everything I wanted: fame, wealth, and most important to me, respect? I would never have chosen to shuffle my priorities around, much less en-dure the earthquake that God seemed to authorize. But in the shaking, I discovered that many of my priorities didn't need reor-ganization as much as they needed elimination.

After all the disruption, I have found hindsight to be not only twenty-twenty, but in some instances, quite humorous as well. Whenever I turn a mental one-eighty degrees, I am usually sur-prised by the events that devastated me at the time, and with a raised eyebrow and a half smirk, I now think to myself, *Ohhhhhhh, so* that's *what God was doing!*

TASTY MORSELS

As I scroll through my mental archives for an example of this, one occasion is yelping, "Pick me! Pick me!"

I had just moved to Nashville, begun my first bus tour, and released a record—all within the span of one week. I might as well have gotten married for good measure—it seemed like the perfect time to throw in one more life-changing event.

My record company had secured me an "opportunity" (code for something that is undesirable, seemingly optional, but really mandatory) with a company that was Web streaming the Dove Awards from backstage. The Doves are to contemporary Christian music what the GRAMMYs are to secular music. As the award winners were whisked offstage and into the publicity room, my job was to type their interview questions and answers, real-time, for the online world to follow. Never was I more thankful for Miss Turner, Intro to Typing, ninth grade. Tap, tap, tapping away, I barely had enough concentration left over to breathe.

This was not exactly how I had imagined my first "appearance" at the Dove Awards. I had trusted my record company that this was good visibility for me as a brand-new recording artist and that perhaps I would garner my own interviews during any breaks in the action. I was game for anything. No task was too small. Whatever it took to get me to where I wanted to go.

I was just beginning to get the hang of the evening when one of the best and brightest artists from the label I had just signed with came through the door. Although we had met on a few occasions and had even hung out at some industry functions together, nothing about me seemed to be ringing a bell for him. As he stepped up to the table, he reached out his hand and asked me how long I had been working as an interviewer. Too embarrassed to remind him that I was a labelmate and *not* a professional interviewer, I sheepishly responded, "Not long." As in, like, the last thirty minutes. To deepen my humiliation, a woman from his entourage later tugged on my arm and asked me if I could get her a Diet Coke. "Uhhh, sure… No problem." *What am I doing here?*

The evening ended about as disappointingly as it started. I left feeling like an outsider, as if the whole event was for people who had somehow figured out how to crack the code of superiority for which I had yet to discover the combination. As I think back to that extravaganza now, however, I no longer shudder with mortification; I smile with relief. Relief that I am no longer controlled by all that. The shimmer and sparkle of the "successful" artists in our town don't dazzle me nearly as much as when I first moved here. I've had my own share of achievements since then, but I'm finally beginning to understand the futility and emptiness of a life that is built solely on such things. Initially there was something mysterious and alluring about the power these performers seemed to have. Seeing the hordes of people lining up for an opportunity to get a mere glimpse of them, I thought that their level of prestige was well worth whatever struggle it would take to get there myself. My thinking was logical but amiss: *If everyone is after them, they must have something I lack—and something I* need *in order to be okay.*

I am not down on success or awards shows. I am not opposed to the respect that well-deserving individuals receive. I am all for beauty and great music, for nights of celebration and photo shoots. I think of Esther whose beauty God used to gain her an entry point to save a nation. I remember David who was described as handsome and ruddy (though God looked at David's heart, not at his appearance). Daniel was smart. Moses was well educated. Solomon was wealthy. Beauty, wits, social status, and a pure heart are not mutually exclusive. Achievement and humility, success and godliness, *can* coexist. But I've learned that the superficial things God uses or allows may be tasty morsels that go down easily and leave a sweet taste in our mouths, but they do little to satisfy our deepest longings.

TRANSFORMED DESIRES

The struggle to matter and the weariness that goes hand in hand with chasing the lure of the world has felt to me like eating cotton candy on an empty stomach. Yet I am still the queen of coming back for more. No matter how many times I'm left wanting, it seems I'm always up for scraping together the last of my nickels and dumping them onto the countertop at the candy store. I'll plunk down the last of them for one more lick on a good lollipop.

But I have to say that even *I* am getting tired. The hope that has sprung eternal is beginning to wane. I'm starting to weary of the emptiness and slight nausea I feel after my wild-goose chases. I'm beginning to believe what God says—not just in my head, but in my heart. The fat has been trimmed away these past few years. God has cut my life down to the bare bones, and I am beginning to discover what truly brings me joy and inner satisfaction.

"Delight yourself in the LORD and he will give you the desires of your heart." As a child I used to love this promise in Psalm 37:4. It seemed like the one magic bean I could swallow, and then God would have to give me everything I ever wanted: *I'll delight in you, and you give me what I want. Deal? Deal.* But I was the only one dealing.

Besides entirely missing the point, I believe I had the interpretation wrong as well. As we delight ourselves in the heart of God, he implants new desires within us. He gives us the *actual desires,* not necessarily the *object* of our desires (though, in his kindness, he often does this as well). I'm starting to get the real point of this verse. It is being borne out in my life. My desires have changed. I have new ones altogether—ones that can be legitimately satisfied.

When I was on the verge of releasing my second record, my goals were significantly different than they were for my first release. I cared a lot less about what an industry had to say about my project and far more about the type of impact it would have on people. Of course, I will be delighted if my record is well received by radio and if the press coverage is glowing, but I will be desperately disappointed if that is all there is. My desires have changed.

Scripture has served as a mirror to my soul, helping me monitor these ever-changing desires. I can often tell where my heart is focused based upon what passages and stories are grabbing my attention. Recently I read about an event in David's life that touched me to my core. A raging and jealous king, Saul was on the hunt, knowing that his kingdom was slipping out of his grasp. David was on the run—as was his custom. He was holed up in a cave—a less-than-royal but sufficient hideout for the time being. Family and friends heard of his whereabouts and came calling: "All those who were in distress or in debt or discontented gathered around him, and he became their leader. About four hundred men were with him" (1 Samuel 22:2).

David became the leader of the broken, while Saul fought to remain foreman of those who had it all together. David's men sought him out, all the way to a damp cave; Saul had to lord his power over his men to keep them. David had a band of four hundred; Saul, an army of thousands. But David knew who he was, and he knew what God had promised him. There was nothing to fear, just wounded and hurting hearts to tend to. He knew how to do this after all those years of lulling his sheep to sleep with the lullabies of his harp and hum. Saul had everything—including the throne—yet was desperately insecure, willing to slaughter as many as it took to retain what he knew deep down he couldn't keep: the kingdom. Saul was blinded by the sparkle of power and prestige and glamour. He spent his days and lost his sleep to keep what he thought he so desperately needed. He was controlled by everything he was supposed to be ruler of.

Is that any different from the clinking of glasses and the worship of fit bodies and the pursuit of the perfect image? These things are here for but a moment. Great effort is required to maintain what is supposed to bring meaning to our lives, yet we only end up grasping for more, desperately afraid that we will one day lose what we're not even convinced we have.

I realized how much God had changed me when I found myself so drawn to this part of David's story. *I will take the four hundred limping and bruised cave dwellers over a sea of packaged and perfect fans any day,* I thought. And this heart-change continues to deepen. I think I will be content to live in relative obscurity if it means that I can genuinely nurse hurting hearts back to health. I will be pleased to fall short of fame and wealth if it means that I will be controlled by nothing; if it means that I can go quietly about the work God gives me to do, free of the "Nashvegas" treadmill that is difficult to get off of and even trickier to stay on.

A respected businessman in town wrote me this e-mail upon my arrival in Nashville: "Kelly, people will force you into their definition of what success is, but this industry's definition is warped! Do you want to impact culture or sell a million units? If you know where you want to be and what is important for you to be involved with, then others and their definitions will not be able to discourage you. You will feel God's pleasure, and that ultimately is so much more valuable than any short-term pleasure derived from some numeric goal."

To feel God's pleasure. I think this is what my heart is ultimately hungering for. Sometimes I grasp for the other things, but I find that they are poor substitutes for what I am longing for deep down: to experience *God's delight in me*. I want to know that my life is pleasing to him and that I'm more than "okay." This is what I crave.

I don't think I would have said this five years ago. Like the cupcakes my mom used to prick with toothpicks to determine if they were done, I needed more time in the oven. I hate to say it, but I *needed* the desert and the trials that God allowed (or ordained) to transform me. All of this has refined my vantage point so that, regardless of how my career plays out, if I spend the majority of my life sloshing water around, holding up the broken and being held up, and if in the end I find Jesus and his secrets—I know I will be so much richer for it.

11

THE ULTIMATE GALA

There are approximately seven inches of snow outside my parents'
home in Virginia, where I am currently attempting to write. And
I say attempting, because my success rate is rather iffy at the
moment. The neighbors are sledding; my dad and my brother are
downstairs playing Ping-Pong; my mom is in the kitchen cooking
something that I'm certain contains at least one of the three evils:
sugar, fat, or salt; my friend is begging me to go with her to the
outlets; and five Starbucks within a two-mile radius are now offering Christmas eggnog lattes…in crimson snowflake cups.

The combination of these distractions and temptations is cruel
and unusual—especially since I am endeavoring to tackle a subject
on which I have only a glimmer of real enlightenment. I am referring to the exchange between Mary and Jesus as the curtain rises
on the wedding scene at Cana. Mary comes to her son, informing

him that the wine has run out. Jesus responds: "Dear woman, why do you involve me?… My time has not yet come" (John 2:4).

Jesus's remarks here have held many Bible scholars—which I most definitely am not—in full nelsons. I have sought several respectable opinions and have come up lacking any authoritative explanation. However, I do think that we can take clues from the rest of Scripture, which clearly indicates that Christ was sent for a very specific purpose: to redeem the world through his death and resurrection. Perhaps this (the Cross) is what he was referring to when he said to Mary, "My time has not yet come." And perhaps when he asked her why she wanted to involve him, he was trying to express to her that there was a much higher purpose for his life than tending to a wedding reception that has run out of wine.

It's impossible to know exactly what Jesus was communicating, but sometimes when it's difficult to grasp the meaning of something, it helps to approach the riddle by defining what it does *not* mean. And this is where I believe we can safely be more emphatic; Jesus did *not* say that his time had come and that, therefore, he should be involved. *This, he obviously did not mean.*

I write these next words with some trepidation because I have a deep respect for Scripture and would never want to propagate error. But I believe that turning water into wine at the wedding in Cana was not part of "the plan" that day. Because, regardless of what Jesus meant when he said that his time had not yet come, it is evident that the time was not at that moment. And for me, this is precisely what gives this passage its unique loveliness and depth. *Jesus involved himself anyway!* He allowed his dramatic statement to simply hang out there while he set about doing the very thing he indicated he was not supposed to do—involve himself.

I believe I will be mining the depths of this interaction for many years to come. Because it tells me that, without forsaking the will of his Father or haphazardly waving a "miracle wand," Jesus set aside his ultimate agenda to supernaturally engage himself in meeting the earthy, temporal, and even decadent needs of the wedding party.

This is profound to me, because my own life is filled with so many Cana-like dilemmas that seem of vital, earth-shattering importance to me, but they pale in comparison with the truly eternal, supernatural, essential things of God. Yet God tends to them. And he extends himself to me. He graciously says, "Why do you involve me?" But in the same breath, he turns to be involved.

I cannot tell you how meaningful this is to me. It suggests that God generously bears with my "emergencies" and grants many of my temporal, fleeting desires, even though they are human and dwarfed in comparison to his glorious, eternal plan. What is perhaps more staggering is that somehow he brings each of us to that plan, even as he detours through our we're-out-of-wine predicaments just as he did at the wedding. When all was said and done that day in Cana, the gazes of the servants, the disciples, Mary—and perhaps others—were turned from the earthly to the supernatural. These common people became tasters of divine wine. They were brought face to face with the grandeur of Christ and his miracle-working power.

Just My Luck

I recall one specific example of this that happened to me almost ten years ago—a seemingly miraculous experience that I had recorded in the pages of my very mundane blue binder. I was headed to Manhattan with Tonia. It was my maiden excursion to the Big Apple, and the first stop on a two-week tour of East Coast cities that I was proudly taking in my trusty Jeep, with no air conditioning, in the height of summer. (My trusty Jeep, by the way, has just been given only six more months to live, er, run.)

The plan was to have dinner in the city with an artist whom I was a huge fan of at the time. We had a mutual friend who knew I was just beginning to get my own musical feet wet and that any time at all with this artist would be a once-in-a-lifetime experience for me. Our friend graciously set up the dinner, which I simply couldn't believe I was going to enjoy. But, sure enough, given my string of luck (which I don't believe in—but if I were to believe in it, I'm quite certain I wouldn't have any), the day after we got to the city, my friend called to tell me that the dinner had been canceled due to an unforeseeable change in this artist's schedule.

I was sick. I ran through my dramatic, self-pitying, "This-always-happens-to-me" rhetoric with Tonia. She sat next to me with an "I'm-really-fine-either-way" look, which is what's so maddening about her. She's always fine either way. It's virtually impossible to ruffle her, while it's highly unlikely you will ever find me *un*ruffled about something. That night, however, I ended up finding a measure of peace in the midst of my disappointment. I distinctly recall lying in bed reminding God that he could still make our dinner happen. I pleaded with him to make it so, to somehow resurrect it, throwing in the traditional caveat, "If it be your will."

The next morning I got up, went Rollerblading, shopped, and mostly forgot about my disappointment. I wore myself right out into the evening, almost collapsing into a seat next to Tonia in one of Broadway's myriad theaters. We watched *Beauty and the Beast,* and I loved it, mainly because it did a thorough job of making me forget about my cancelled dinner and all my disappointment. Happy and contented, Tonia and I strolled out of the theater into the dazzling excitement of Times Square on a Friday night. Thousands upon thousands of bustling people traversed our path. We had left a cozy theater and plunged into a sea of what felt like millions of people, when suddenly—and as implausible as anything could ever be—the artist I'd been slated to have dinner with literally bumped into me. (Incidentally, we had been introduced a handful of times, so when I spontaneously called out her name, she knew enough about me to know that I wasn't some crazed, psycho-fan—though what she didn't know about me was that, essentially, I was a crazed, psycho-fan. So she stopped.)

Bewilderment and shock came across her face. She had totally forgotten about the dinner with friends of a friend (us) and simply couldn't believe what was happening—that we had "randomly" run into each other in the middle of Manhattan on the craziest night of the week. We stared at each other with mouths gaping, as if to say, "We could spend the next million years trying to orchestrate this one, and we'd still need ten thousand more to make it happen." She grabbed my playbill, wrote down all of her information, and then invited us to her home for coffee the next morning.

I will never forget getting into the cab that night, clutching my playbill and staring out the window, speechless. As far as I could understand it, God had peered down from heaven and had somehow perfectly aligned the paths of what must have looked like two tiny specks so that they would converge at just the right second and on just the right minuscule plot of earth—all because it was important to me. But even more important, I believe he orchestrated this incredible event so that my gaze would be lifted to him. Because he wanted me to see his power and his love for me.

Much like the wedding that had run out of wine, my cancelled dinner probably wasn't all that tragic of an event in the scheme of things. Although I was disappointed, I'm doubtful that it was one of the eternal, weighty, ultimate concerns of God. Perhaps if I could have heard his voice, he would have told me that there were much deeper and more dismal things going on in the world than not getting to have dinner with a celebrity and that I needed to see my situation from a more eternal, spiritual perspective. Perhaps he would even have asked me why I was involving him in such trivial and incidental matters.

Yet he arranged it all. He tended to my desires. He took time—whatever that looks like to God—and in the middle of New York City, meticulously arranged for my path to intersect with the very person I wanted to meet. He does this kind of thing all the time. Every day, I'm convinced. He is so gracious to us, just as he was to the wedding guests in Cana. He is so willing to become involved in what is important to us, to deal in the temporal even though he is concerned with the eternal. To lift our eyes to him so that we can join him on a more lasting level. This is why he came to earth, and to a manger, and to a cross, and to our hearts—and even to a wedding.

THE GOD WHO COMES TO US

This fact is obvious by now, I know: Jesus was an attending guest at the wedding in Cana. He was invited, and he came. But these fairly inconsequential details often end up being noteworthy in the end. They are noteworthy to me because I would think that the Son of God had other more important things to do—a more universe-impacting agenda that didn't include spending precious time at a wedding reception. I suppose my response exposes the fact that I have a hard time embracing the humanity of Jesus—that he truly came to earth fully God, but also fully man. That he routinely engaged in so many of the celebrations and gatherings and meals and holidays and weddings that we do.

But it also reveals my struggle to recognize him as a God who would gladly come to my wedding or would meet me at a well, or on a hillside, or on the water. I tend to view it otherwise: That *I* am the one who is always pursuing *Him*. Even while studying Scripture, praying, solemnly sitting in the sanctuary, or looking for a remnant of his glory in the rappelling spider that has spun its web across my path, I tend to think of God as hard to find.

Ironically, however, he is not the One who needs to be found. I may seek him endlessly, but it is *I* who need to be found. And I have already been found—by him. A simple acknowledgment of this profound fact, and a deeper understanding that I have not gone to him, but he has come to me, would probably make a world of difference in my relationship with him. I imagine I would experience less angst, because to be found is an amazingly comforting thing. For if I am looking for someone, it is because I want him; but if someone is looking for me, it is because *I* am wanted. And this is most definitely at the core—ironically enough—of everything I want. To be wanted and pursued regardless of what I know about myself. To be known fully by God and to find him coming to me whether or not I put my spiritual best foot forward.

An exchange between Jesus and a centurion in Matthew's gospel has brought me enormous comfort in this regard. The centurion's servant was suffering at home, paralyzed, so the centurion approached Jesus on the servant's behalf. Before the officer could even ask Jesus for help, Jesus uttered a phrase that becomes more magnificent to me as the account unfolds, "*I will come* and heal him" (Matthew 8:7, KJV, emphasis added).

The centurion, however, humbly assured Jesus that he didn't need to come to the servant but could simply say the word and the suffering man would be healed. Jesus held up the centurion's great faith as an example to all his followers, then he promised that the servant would be healed just as the centurion had envisioned.

After having read this passage more times than I can number, I was struck by a thought I'd never had before: Jesus knew that all he had to do was "say the word" from where he stood, and the paralyzed man would be healed. Why, then, did Jesus offer at the outset to go to the servant in person? One of many possible reasons is that Jesus was willing to meet the centurion's needs (healing his servant) regardless of what he believed could happen or how much faith he had. Jesus was going to heal the servant one way or another. The healing was not contingent upon the measure of faith the centurion possessed. If he had faith enough to believe that all Jesus had to do was speak healing from afar, then Jesus would speak. But if he thought it necessary for Jesus to come home with him and physically touch his servant, then Jesus was willing to come.

Jesus comes to me and to you, and has already come to all of us, regardless of our faith or lack thereof. He doesn't come because we have what it takes or have figured out a way to manage our lifestyle or behavior, or have attained the great faith of the centurion. Rather, he is willing to come before we even ask—because of his love and grace. This is the very definition of grace: It comes to meet us wherever we are.

RELENTLESS PURSUIT

Before moving to Nashville, I commuted for several years, flying in every few months and staying with the Brown family, six delightful people I had never met until I showed up on their doorstep with my bags and guitar. They had agreed to take me in for two weeks, and so I wonder if you might consider it an imposition if I told you that I ended up living with them on and off for three years. I got very close to this family, as you can imagine, and they got close to me—probably closer than they ever dreamed or desired. I have to say that living with them was one of the most incredibly meaningful experiences of my young adult life. I learned a lot about southern living and homemade desserts and diapers and, especially, boys.

J. Mac and Julie Brown have four sons, all under the age of seven at the time. I learned about the sweetness of brotherhood and how the same genes can produce vastly different personalities. I witnessed firsthand how a three-year-old can stop you dead in your tracks with some blurb of wisdom he innocently murmurs while smearing jelly across his shirt. In addition, I got crash courses in coloring and blocks and pregnant cats that can't think of anywhere else to bring life into the world except underneath a bunk bed. But most important, I learned about the hearts of children.

The Brown boys didn't judge me by Music Row standards. They had no measuring stick for "cool" or famous or successful. They didn't accept or reject me based on my ability or merits or on how white my teeth were. They loved me...so they pursued me. They came to me.

Some of my favorite and most grounding moments during my first few years in Nashville consisted of driving into the Browns' driveway after a long day or a week away. Invariably the boys would be outside playing, and as soon as they spotted my Jeep, they would spring off their next-door neighbor's trampoline like pieces of popcorn catapulted into the air, with their superman capes unfurling in the wind. They would accost me like bees swarming a spoonful of honey. Barnes was notorious for offering up some sort of freshly plucked flower (weed); Miller would hardly say hello before throwing out several well-crafted reasons as to why we needed to immediately head to the creek; Watts was the most affectionate, jumping into my arms and smothering me with kisses; and Liam would hold up both arms, as limp and helpless looking as possible, signaling that he might not make it to his next birthday if I didn't pick him up and hold him right that minute.

This daily reception put a lot of things in perspective for me. Regardless of magazine reviews, great or shaky performances, stressful travel, good hair days, or bad skin days, the Brown boys remained the same. My career achievements or failings had no bearing on whether they would be excited to see me or would come to greet me with loving enthusiasm.

Believing that God comes to me much the same way has been tough, mainly because I have subscribed to the notion that doing the wrong things prompts God's absence, while doing the right things ensures his presence. Though I still believe that elements of this are valid on certain levels, I am learning that an entirely different sphere exists where things simply aren't that neat, and don't make that much sense, and are ultimately held together only by God's unmerited favor toward us. The Jesus who came to earth, to the wedding at Cana, to our own hearts shows us that we can rest in his faithful pursuit of us, regardless of our finest virtues or darkest inclinations. His coming has nothing to do with us; it is all about him, and his relentlessly loving heart.

Unlike the complicated exchange that Mary had with Jesus, we will never have to wonder if Jesus's decision to involve himself in our lives is part of "the plan." Because now we *know* it is. His hour *has* come. He has come to the cross; he has extended forgiveness to us; he has involved himself in our lives forever! Amen.

Having said all this, I want to mention one small thing that completes the circle of Jesus's coming, something that is found in the opening line of this magnificent story of his turning water into wine: "On the third day a wedding took place…and Jesus and his disciples had also been invited to the wedding" (John 2:1-2)

Jesus was *invited.*

And so if any part of his coming is up to us, I believe it lies within our invitation. Though even our invitation wasn't necessary to draw Jesus down from heaven, or to the cross, or to our doorstep. But I do believe an invitation is essential for him to enter our hearts. He will not come into our inner sanctuary unless we ask him. So even though his coming has nothing whatsoever to do with us, it also has everything to do with us.

ETERNAL BLESSINGS

When I began writing this book more than a year and a half ago, I had no idea how much I would be living it out. One of my closest friends here in Nashville says that the manifestation of this writing in my life has been a terrible and wonderful thing to watch. Terrible, because it has been painful and has dismantled many of my preconceived beliefs and cherished dreams; wonderful, because more of Jesus is now visible. God has taken great delight in confounding me, my friend says.

I believe this is true. These past few years have overturned many of my previous notions. I have learned that the value and quality of my life does not depend on the glamour and successes of a particular career path. Glass clinking is but for a moment, but water drawing delivers miraculous and eternal rewards. I have learned that servanthood is not about bucking up under a list of spiritual "chores," but instead, it is about the posture of my heart toward God. And I have learned that obedience cannot be measured out; it only counts in full—when it's "to the brim." Any blessings that come as a result of my obedience and service are not self-righteous medals that I can wear on my lapel; they are soul-filling secrets from Jesus that I am privileged and blessed to know.

How disheartening it was to discover, at first, that I am only capable of water in, water out. My best efforts amount to nothing more. But how glorious and comforting it is to discover that grace has met me at exactly the place where my mundane efforts have ended in water and has turned them miraculously into wine. The pressure is off now. I don't have to strain and strive with every muscle in my soul to make myself presentable to God. For he has already come to the door of my heart. He is already here.

As I sew up my final thoughts, I think of the way I began this book—at a wedding. An event I certainly would have avoided as a kid but would now jump at the chance to attend. It makes me think of my youngest sister Katie's wedding that we celebrated just a few months ago. Her marriage officially made Brad my first (and, therefore, favorite) Italian brother-in-law. It makes me wonder what my own wedding will look like, if I am blessed in such a way.

But mostly it makes me think of the ultimate gala that underlies all of redemption. The wedding in which Jesus Christ is the groom and we are his bride. The wedding Paul spoke of in Romans, where Jesus actually weds his church. It is a wedding so glorious and unfathomable that Paul referred to it as a mystery. And we are invited to get swept up in this mystery, this wedding, if we will simply extend our own invitation—an invitation that asks the same Jesus who turned water into wine at Cana to turn sin into righteousness, and penalty into forgiveness, and darkness into light in our hearts. This invitation will take us to a wedding far beyond Cana, to a wedding in the heavens where water turning to wine will be just a shadow of the transformation God has done in our hearts.

Come...dance with me there.

Notes

Chapter 3

1. Watchman Nee, *The Normal Christian Life* (Wheaton, IL: Tyndale, 1977).
2. C. S. Lewis, quoted in *The Complete C. S. Lewis Signature Classics* (San Francisco: HarperSanFrancisco, 2002), 81.

Chapter 6

1. Dallas Willard, *The Divine Conspiracy: Rediscovering Our Hidden Life in God* (New York: HarperCollins, 1998), xiii.
2. Willard, *The Divine Conspiracy*, 13.

ABOUT THE AUTHOR

KELLY MINTER is a singer-songwriter who has performed and toured with Bebo Norman, Watermark, SONICFLOOd, 4Him, Anointed, and Newsong. Kelly has also released two nationally distributed records, *Good Day* and *Wrestling the Angels*. Although her platform initially came through her music, Kelly is also known for her speaking abilities, and she now speaks frequently in colleges and church settings.

Kelly has a unique ability to blend her own musical style into a worship setting while also communicating her faith. Through her life's message of music, speaking, and the written word, Kelly challenges her generation to find ultimate truth and life-sustaining faith. Kelly is a spokesperson for World Vision and lives in Nashville, Tennessee.

FOR BOOKINGS OR SPEAKING ENGAGEMENTS CONTACT:

Muse and Associates
Pamela Muse
115 Penn Warren
Suite 300–#387
Brentwood, TN 37027
Phone: 615-777-2211